Praise for *When Did We Start Forgetting God?*

Mark Galli thinks we have an evangelical crisis. So we'd be wise to listen. He shows how in the long-standing tension between "doing" and "being," we have too many Marthas and not enough Marys. But we couldn't cure this crisis with a thousand sermons on how to have a better marriage or job or a bigger bank account. Instead, Mark shares ancient and biblical wisdom that can help us remember where we left God and how to find him again.

COLLIN HANSEN

Editorial director for The Gospel Coalition, coauthor of *A God-Sized Vision: Revival Stories That Stretch and Stir*, and editor of *Our Secular Age: Ten Years of Reading and Applying Charles Taylor*

Mark Galli gets it! As a Christian committed to both vertical and horizontal planes of the Christian message—righteousness and justice, embracing the grace of God and expressing the love of God—Mark offers an excellent rubric for those of us committed to changing the world in the name of Jesus. This book reminds us of a sacred balance that must be maintained where our prophetic activism never trumps our vertical pursuit of righteousness. We must love Jesus more than we love doing justice in his name. Thank you, Mark!

SAMUEL RODRIGUEZ

Lead pastor of New Season Church, president of the National Hispanic Christian Leadership Conference, author of *You Are Next!*, and executive producer of the movie *Breakthrough*

For those of us who have been at all shaped by American evangelicalism (or even ex-evangelicalism), *When Did We Start Forgetting God?* will challenge our assumptions and oversimplistic thinking about what the church is and what it is for. Galli calls the church to faithfulness and catholicity in practical and profound ways. Drawing upon the wisdom of the historic church, he casts a vision for the place of preaching, prayer, worship, the sacraments, and the community in the renewal of the church in the twenty-first century. This book is helpful, rich, and vital for any who care about and want to serve the church in America.

TISH HARRISON WARREN
Priest in the Anglican Church in North America; writer-in-residence at Church of the Ascension, Pittsburgh, PA; and author of *Liturgy of the Ordinary*

WHEN DID WE START FORGETTING GOD?

THE ROOT OF THE EVANGELICAL CRISIS AND HOPE FOR THE FUTURE

MARK GALLI

TYNDALE
MOMENTUM®

The Tyndale nonfiction imprint

Visit Tyndale online at www.tyndale.com.

Visit Tyndale Momentum online at www.tyndalemomentum.com.

TYNDALE, Tyndale's quill logo, *Tyndale Momentum*, and the Tyndale Momentum logo are registered trademarks of Tyndale House Publishers. Tyndale Momentum is the nonfiction imprint of Tyndale House Publishers, Carol Stream, Illinois.

When Did We Start Forgetting God?: The Root of the Evangelical Crisis and Hope for the Future

Cover design by David Carlson/Studio Gearbox

Interior designed by Julie Chen

Edited by Jonathan Schindler

For information about special discounts for bulk purchases, please contact Tyndale House Publishers at csresponse@tyndale.com, or call 1-800-323-9400.

Library of Congress Cataloging-in-Publication Data

Names: Galli, Mark, author.
Title: When did we start forgetting God? : the root of the evangelical crisis and hope for our future / Mark Galli.
Description: Carol Stream, Illinois : Tyndale House Publishers, 2020. | Includes bibliographical references.
Identifiers: LCCN 2019042772 (print) | LCCN 2019042773 (ebook) | ISBN 9781414373614 (trade paperback) | ISBN 9781414384436 (kindle edition) | ISBN 9781496419057 (epub) | ISBN 9781496419040 (epub)
Subjects: LCSH: Evangelistic work. | Evangelicalism. | Christian life. | Spirituality—Christianity.
Classification: LCC BV3770 .G35 2020 (print) | LCC BV3770 (ebook) | DDC 277.3/083—dc23
LC record available at https://lccn.loc.gov/2019042772
LC ebook record available at https://lccn.loc.gov/2019042773

Printed in the United States of America

26 25 24 23 22 21 20
7   6   5   4   3   2   1

CONTENTS

Foreword *vii*

Introduction *1*

PART 1: THE CRISIS

CHAPTER 1 Monomaniacs for God *11*

CHAPTER 2 We Have Forgotten God *27*

PART 2: THE CHURCH

CHAPTER 3 Rethinking the Church:
The Problem with a Missional
Mind-Set *45*

CHAPTER 4 Rethinking the Church:
A Biblical Picture *53*

CHAPTER 5 Rethinking the Church:
A More Balanced Diet *71*

CHAPTER 6 The Focus of Worship *83*

CHAPTER 7 What Ever Happened to
Communion? *93*

CHAPTER 8 Back to the Bible *101*

CHAPTER 9 And Now, the Star of Our
Show . . . *111*

CHAPTER 10 Making Small Groups Bigger
in Purpose *123*

PART 3: DEEPENING DESIRE

CHAPTER 11 Shaping Desire *137*

CHAPTER 12 Love and Loathing *149*

CHAPTER 13 The World, the Flesh,
the Devil, and Religion *155*

CHAPTER 14 No Other Gods *171*

CHAPTER 15 Remember the Sabbath *183*

CHAPTER 16 The Bible Tells Me So *191*

CHAPTER 17 Contemplative Prayer *201*

CHAPTER 18 Suffering *209*

CHAPTER 19 Confession *217*

CHAPTER 20 Loving the Neighbor While
Loving God *227*

Acknowledgments *237*

Notes *239*

About the Author *245*

FOREWORD

I AM GLAD FOR THIS BOOK, *When Did We Start Forgetting God?* It pointedly addresses critical issues throughout the entire Christian community and especially for evangelicals in North America. As editor in chief of the evangelical flagship magazine *Christianity Today*, Mark Galli has been in a strategic position to view the multiple strands of evangelical faith around the world and most specifically in North America. My guess is that he is on a first-name basis with all the major players in American evangelicalism. Hence, when he speaks, we do well to listen.

Galli speaks to us not as some outside critic but as one on the inside who loves the church and loves the evangelical movement in all its manifold expressions. Galli believes that American evangelicalism is in deep crisis, and he is concerned to speak to what he considers the most critical issues at hand. He takes contemporary evangelicalism to task on multiple fronts.

As I read his passionate analysis, several phrases kept bubbling to the surface of my mind—phrases that I hope will help us draw near to the heartbeat of this book.

One phrase that immediately came to my mind was *biblically rooted*. In saying this, I am not suggesting that Galli is a

Biblicist who scours the Bible for verses to proof-text every jot and tittle of his observations. To be sure, Scripture passages abound, but they serve the purpose of allowing the biblical worldview to inform his experiences and teachings. Galli is, I believe, seeking to follow the biblical path wherever it leads.

Another phrase that kept surfacing was *bold critique*. The word *bold* is carefully chosen here. Galli does not spare cherished organizations in the evangelical movement. For example, he provides a biting critique of both social justice advocates and those who uncritically embrace a chief executive with "blatantly immoral behavior and speech." I think it best for me to leave the specific names and groups for you to discover in the text itself. But there is far more than critique here. Galli provides us with a thoughtful historical perspective from the great evangelical awakenings in North America from the 1730s onward. Especially helpful is his careful discussion of the 1801 Cane Ridge Communion Revivals in Kentucky. For Galli, these provide us with something of a paradigm for his hoped-for corrective.

A third phrase that repeatedly came to my mind was *evangelical fidelity*. Galli seeks to restore evangelicalism to a robust faithfulness in both devotion and practice. I am glad he has not given up on the word *evangelical*. It is, after all, a deeply biblical word, and it has a glowing history at critical junctures in the Christian story throughout the ages. To be sure, contemporary expressions are more clouded, but the jury is still out on the future direction for evangelical faith. So I applaud Galli's efforts to call evangelicalism to a purer, more faithful future.

Far and away the most persistent phrase that kept echoing in my mind throughout my reading of *When Did We Start Forgetting God?* was *longing desire*. Galli is calling all of us—personally and corporately—to a flaming love for God with all our heart, soul, mind, and strength. He urges us to keep first things first and second things second.

Galli's use of the term *desire* is taken from a long and honored tradition of Christian moral formation. Perhaps a recent experiment of mine will help unpack what he is after here. At the outset of the New Year I sought God's guidance for a prayer that might carry me through the entire year. After a few days the prayer that emerged was a simple four-part petition:

Lord Jesus, please . . .
purify my heart,
renew my mind,
sanctify my imagination,
enlarge my soul.
Amen.

Most often I will pray in this way over a morning cup of coffee. At times I may sense a divine invitation to linger over one particular area. Instruction or guidance may be given, and, perhaps, confession from me. Most of all is the stillness of a familiar friendship. I seek to pray in this way even when the intentions of my heart are far from pure. Sometimes—not always, but sometimes—this prayer will follow me throughout the various activities of my day. *Purify . . . renew . . . sanctify . . . enlarge.*

I am now eight months into this simple experiment in

prayer. And one change I am noticing is a gentle shifting in my desires. Some desires are dropping away and others are rising up. For example, ever so slowly I feel myself drawn to experience those life-giving words of Frederick W. Faber:

> *Only to sit and think of God—*
> *Oh, what a joy it is!*
> *To think the thought, to breathe the Name—*
> *Earth has no higher bliss!*

Stepping further back in Christian history, I am finding myself more recently attracted to the experience that Catherine of Siena describes in her *Dialogue* where she has God speaking to her, saying, "The soul cannot live without love. She always wants to love something because love is the stuff she is made of, and through love I created her." Of course, I am far from entering into all the dimensions of living that are described here, but I desire such a life more now than when I first began my little prayer experiment at the beginning of the year.

Isn't this what we all desire . . . or at least desire to desire? Through all the vicissitudes of life, our desire is for this white-hot love for God to be our very first order of business. Nothing is more central. Nothing is more important. Nothing is more critical. Not good deeds. Not faithful service in the church. Not missional labor in the name of Christ. Nothing. We love God alone. We adore God alone. We worship God alone. We are blinded to all other loyalties.

Richard J. Foster

INTRODUCTION

IT'S HARD TO KNOW when the current evangelical crisis started, because one characteristic feature of the movement is its relentless self-criticism. Evangelicalism is a reform movement, and one object of evangelicals is to reform themselves.

I do remember when I became aware of a personal crisis that gave me insight into the challenge we all face. It came in dribs and drabs of insight, like the morning I sat down in my home office, wake-up coffee in hand, to once again try to kick-start my daily devotions. It was early winter, and from my easy chair I looked out on the trees in our neighborhood. The morning sky was just being lit by the rising sun, and the bare limbs of the trees stood out in stark outline.

Next came a thought that may be trite as a metaphor but startling in its meaning. The dead limbs pictured the state of my spiritual life. My Christian life was, well, lifeless. I didn't have any yearning to know and love God. I wasn't angry with him. I didn't doubt his existence. I wasn't wrestling with the problem of evil. I was being a faithful Christian as best I knew how. But it occurred to me that I didn't feel any love for God.

As I sipped my coffee, my mind slowly got in gear. I also realized that although I prayed and read Scripture regularly, even if in spurts, not much in my life would be different if I didn't pray and read my Bible. I was living as a practical atheist. My personal relationship with God did not really affect anything I did or said except the formal trappings of Christianity. I was at the time managing editor of *Christianity Today*, so naturally I edited and wrote a lot of things that were Christian to the core. But I realized that if I never prayed again, I could still be a very good editor at a Christian publication and a very good church member at my local parish. I knew how to get along with others, manage staff, work with my superiors, interact with fellow church members, get things done, and so forth. But prayer wasn't necessary to do all that. Those were all learned skills that had more or less become good habits. My personal relationship with God really didn't make any difference.

My next thought was, *Well, if I call myself a Christian, I should have a greater love for God and desire to know him more deeply. Perhaps I should pray for that.* And yet that morning, like others, it occurred to me that I wasn't sure I wanted that. I recognized this was an odd admission for a person who claimed to be a Christian. But there it was. I didn't think I really *wanted* to love God more.

I'd immersed myself in enough Scripture and Christian theology to know that there was no greater desire than to yearn for God, no greater joy or happiness than to know God with increasing intimacy. And yet I had to admit that as I looked at those bare limbs and into my cold heart, I had little to no interest in that.

I realized at that moment that there was no hiding all this from God and that God had known the state of my heart and my will for some time and was patiently and mercifully waiting for me to see it for myself. That's when I also realized that the most honest prayer was simply "Lord, help me to want to love you."

There is a danger to universalizing one's personal experience to apply to others, let alone an entire body of believers. But I actually believe it worked the other way. For some decades now, as evidenced in my writing, I've believed that American Christianity has been less and less interested in God and more and more in doing good things for God. We've learned how to be effective for him to the point that we don't really need him any longer. It was that continuing concern that finally took hold of me, making me realize that this was not just someone else's crisis but a crisis we all share. Embedded as I have been in evangelical Christianity, I was particularly concerned about my own tribe.

And I've not been alone in thinking there is an evangelical crisis. If I were to pick a moment when the current crisis started emerging in our consciousness, I'd point to the 1995 publication of Dave Tomlinson's *The Post-Evangelical*. He described the book's genesis as two years earlier when, at the Greenbelt Festival in Britain, a friend made a passing reference to "we post-evangelicals." Although he wasn't sure what that meant, Tomlinson decided to figure it out since the term resonated with him and his friends. The book, in his words, is a "pastoral essay directed at those (and there are many) . . .

who struggle with restrictions in evangelical theology, spirituality and church culture."[1]

The book made a big splash in Britain, and the like-minded in America began to take notice. From this and other influences arose the Emergent church movement, which sought, among other things, to adapt evangelical theology to postmodern sensibilities. Perhaps the most well-known attempt was Brian McLaren's New Kind of Christian trilogy, begun in 2001, which blossomed into *A New Kind of Christianity* in 2010. By the publication of the latter book, McLaren was not merely questioning evangelicalism but also orthodox Christianity. For him and many other Emergent leaders, the crisis of evangelicalism was also the crisis of traditional Christianity. Both, as McLaren argued, were mired in the spirit of "modernity," theological rigidity, and a literal reading of Scripture and were cold to mystery, more interested in proclaiming answers than in "living the questions."

McLaren's "disillusionment" was intensified by the increasing alignment of conservative Christians with the politics of the right.[2] Fast-forward to November 9, 2016, the day after Donald Trump was elected president, and the disillusionment had spread and turned into anger for many evangelical leaders when we were told that 81 percent of white voters who identified as "evangelical" voted for Trump.

Fuller Theological Seminary president Mark Labberton summarized the crisis of evangelicalism at a national gathering of evangelical leaders at Wheaton College in 2018. He called it "political dealing," and he castigated evangelicals for grasping at political power, for racism, for nationalism, and for a lack of concern for the poor.[3] As is clear, he was only talking about conservative evangelicals, but to him and many evangelical leaders, it is these evangelicals who constitute *the* crisis of evangelicalism today.

There is no question that the crisis today is more intense than it has ever been, with many evangelicals (usually those who want to distance themselves from anyone who supports Donald Trump) dropping that label, preferring to be known as "followers of Jesus" or "red-letter Christians" or just "Christians." That discomfort with the name has been around for years, starting with those who felt more attuned to labels like *post-evangelical* or *Emergent*. So troublesome are these developments that InterVarsity Press commissioned a book devoted to the meaning and future of the movement: *Still Evangelical?: Insiders Reconsider Political, Social, and Theological Meaning* (a book to which I was a contributor).[4]

Of course, others have located the crisis at the other end of the political and theological spectrum and did so some twenty years earlier in *The Compromised Church: The Present Evangelical Crisis*, an anthology with contributions by Mark Dever, Al Mohler, and Phil Ryken, among others. For these writers, the evangelical church had become shallow theologically, biblically, and in its worship. Their views also have a lot to commend themselves.

Another view of the crisis comes from journalist and historian Molly Worthen. In *Apostles of Reason: The Crisis of Authority in American Evangelicalism*, she argues that evangelicalism is rife with contradictions and confusion because the movement has never had a single authority to guide its life and faith.[5]

This may have been an insight to nonevangelicals, but it was hardly a revelation to those within the movement. This lack of structured authority is the great strength and weakness of evangelicalism. Having only the Bible and each person's reading of it has allowed evangelicalism to be a dynamic movement that shapes the faith attractively to each generation and each culture. But that lack of a central authority inevitably creates arguments and divisions and, therefore, an ongoing crisis in some ways.

These are but a few of the crises that those inside and outside the movement name, and each of the critics has been right in more than one respect. As editor in chief of *Christianity Today* and as someone who has been embedded in the culture of evangelicalism for over half a century, I've not only heard these many complaints, but I also recognize the measure of truth in each of them. They are not to be dismissed with a sweep of the hand.

There is indeed a political crisis (but in my view it's on the right *and* the left). And a crisis of racism (certainly among whites but also increasingly among minorities). And a theological crisis. And a biblical crisis. And a crisis in worship (and not just because of thin worship songs). A crisis in marriage and family. A crisis in evangelism. A crisis in social justice. A crisis in pastoral care. A crisis in discipleship. And on it goes.

Along the way, we've seen increasing predictions of evangelicalism's demise. Ten years ago, the late blogger Michael Spencer sparked one of the first social media conversations about the viability of evangelicalism with his essay "My Prediction: The Coming Evangelical Collapse." Among other things, he said this:

This collapse, will, I believe, herald the arrival of an anti-Christian chapter of the post-Christian West and will change the way tens of millions of people see the entire realm of religion. Intolerance of Christianity will rise to levels many of us have not believed possible in our lifetimes, and public policy will become particularly hostile towards evangelical Christianity, increasingly seeing it as the opponent of the good of individuals and society.

The response of evangelicals to this new environment will be a revisiting of the same rhetoric and reactions we've seen since the beginnings of the current culture war in the 1980s. The difference will be that millions of evangelicals will quit: quit their churches, quit their adherence to evangelical distinctives and quit resisting the rising tide of the culture.

Many who will leave evangelicalism will leave for no religious affiliation at all. Others will leave for atheistic or agnostic secularism, with a strong personal rejection of Christian belief and Christian influence. Many of our children and grandchildren are going to abandon ship, and many will do so saying "good riddance."[6]

I was skeptical at the time he wrote this and said so in print. But today I admit that Spencer was more right than wrong. Recent events and surveys bear out many of his predictions. We truly are in a moment of crisis in American evangelicalism.

To be clear, it doesn't matter to me if, as many predict, the movement known as American evangelicalism fades away with the sunset. God has raised up many reform movements since the Day of Pentecost and has seen many die—some of which I suspect he has killed off. If evangelicalism fades away, he will in his mercy raise up another movement that will revive his people. The future of the church in America does not hinge on the health of evangelicalism; it hinges on the power of God. I'd say we're in good hands.

That being said, American evangelicalism has had a unique beginning, one that energized it and carried it along for two centuries and more. And it has been one of the most revolutionary movements in church history, changing the face not only of North American Christianity, but with the nineteenth-century missionary movement, the entire globe. This history has many troubling elements, as many have noted. This is not surprising because it is a movement full of sinners. But God has been good and has nonetheless used it to enable people from all walks of life and every corner of the world to know the unsurpassable grace of Jesus Christ.

Still, contemporary evangelicalism is in serious trouble. Actually, its crisis is the same one that afflicts all Christianity in America. At the risk of hubris and of merely adding one more item to the seemingly endless list of crises, in this book I suggest that one crisis lies at the heart of what ails large swaths of the American church. Aleksandr Solzhenitsyn named it in his speech upon receiving the Templeton Prize for Progress in Religion in 1983. He was talking about Western culture when he said it, but I apply it to the American church, evangelical and not:

We have forgotten God.

PART 1

THE CRISIS

CHAPTER 1

MONOMANIACS
FOR GOD

It seems absurd to say we have forgotten God, when God is on our lips so much of the time. While the numbers are slightly down from previous decades, Americans worship, pray, read their Bibles, and say in polls that religion is "very important" significantly more than do people in other developed nations. If anything, evangelicals talk about God so much that many in the culture are sick of our God-talk, especially when God's name is invoked in the public square to support one political cause or another. So how can I say we have forgotten God?

Let me begin in part 1 by picturing what the church looks like when it *hasn't* forgotten God. From there I will look specifically at how evangelicalism has slowly but surely displaced God from the center of its attention.

In part 2, I will look at the state of the evangelical church, starting with a three-chapter argument that critiques the most prominent view of the church while suggesting an alternative. After that, I'll show how in each aspect of church life—worship, preaching, small groups, and so forth—we are tempted to cast our eyes away from God and upon ourselves.

In part 3, I'll suggest some of the contours of a life of utter devotion to God, as well as some ways we might begin that long and hard and fruitful journey.

But first, what a church that hasn't forgotten God looks like. To put it succinctly, a church that has not forgotten God exhibits one principal characteristic: a desire for God—a desire so intense it sometimes looks like drunkenness or even madness.

The first place to go looking for a picture of this passion is Scripture.

DESIRE FROM BEGINNING TO END

The most vivid example of such desire is King David. David was known as a man of action, a military leader, a nation's king, busy with the affairs of state. He is also famous for his extramarital affair with Bathsheba and the subsequent murder of her husband. But the one characteristic that seems to have earned him the label of "a man after [God's] own heart" (Acts 13:22) was that he sought God wholeheartedly.

Psalm 63 expresses this most eloquently:

O God, you are my God;
    I earnestly search for you.
My soul thirsts for you;
    my whole body longs for you
in this parched and weary land
    where there is no water.
I have seen you in your sanctuary
    and gazed upon your power and glory.
Your unfailing love is better than life itself;
    how I praise you!
I will praise you as long as I live,
    lifting up my hands to you in prayer.
You satisfy me more than the richest feast.
    I will praise you with songs of joy.

PSALM 63:1-5

Believing that God's presence was especially to be found in the Temple, David also prayed,

The one thing I ask of the LORD—
    the thing I seek most—
is to live in the house of the LORD all the days of my life,
    delighting in the LORD's perfections
    and meditating in his Temple.

PSALM 27:4

Of course, David isn't the only psalmist to yearn for God's palpable presence. Psalm 42 was written by "the descendants of Korah" and famously begins

As the deer longs for streams of water,
    so I long for you, O God.
I thirst for God, the living God.

PSALM 42:1-2

These examples could be multiplied, as any reader of the Psalms knows. The psalmists were driven by a desire to know God. Not just to know his will. Not just to do his will. Not just to be wise. Not just to be righteous. But to *know God*, to be with God, to bask in his presence.

Persons of a stoic nature, like me, are tempted to assume such passion is only for highly emotional personalities. Frankly, at times David and the other psalmists seem like emotional wrecks, either lamenting their sorry state or begging desperately for divine aid or longing passionately for God. My instinct is to tell them to just calm down.

But this over-the-top drive to know and love God is found throughout Scripture, which makes me question my stoicism. For example, we see it also in Isaiah the prophet: "In the night I search for you; in the morning I earnestly seek you" (26:9). We see it in Paul: "Everything else is worthless when compared with the infinite value of knowing Christ Jesus my Lord. For his sake I have discarded everything else, counting it all as garbage, so that I could gain Christ and become one with him" (Philippians 3:8-9). And we see it in Jesus' life and ministry—not so much in his yearning to be one with God (that would be absurd for the one in whom God fully dwells) but in his teaching, especially in what he said was the greatest commandment: "You must love the LORD your God with all your heart, all your soul, all your mind, and all your strength" (Mark 12:30). That pretty much covers the emotional, spiritual, mental, and physical landscape of human life.

To put it another way, Jesus told us we are to be mono-maniacs for God, people whose lives are so obsessed with knowing and loving God that some people might wonder about our sanity. Like Francis of Assisi, whose father was so startled by his efforts to follow Jesus radically that his father locked him in the family cellar until he came to his senses. Like Jesus, whose family thought he was "out of his mind" (Mark 3:21).

Again, people like me—who strive to keep our emotions in check, to navigate life on an even keel, to take things in stride—try to squirm out of this by saying that this first and greatest commandment is merely about obeying God's commands. We demonstrate our love for God by caring for others in very practical ways—doing favors for friends, listening attentively to troubled coworkers, serving at the food pantry, and maybe even standing in a prayer vigil at an abortion clinic or joining a protest march against racial injustice. Doing stuff that helps others—that's what it means to love God.

That's certainly part of it (see 1 John 5:3!). But here's the rub: Jesus didn't say that loving our neighbor is the way we show that we love God. He said the first commandment is to love God, and then he announced a second commandment—as if in a different category—which is to love others. This second commandment was not a commentary on the first.

Add to that the unique character of the first commandment. There is something extraordinary about the love of God. We're commanded to love God with the complete range of emotion, with the full measure of spiritual fervor, with unending intellectual effort, and with every calorie of energy.

Jesus, as was his custom, was using hyperbole, because if we were to love God like this we wouldn't have anything left for the neighbor. But the point is made. Jesus was simply putting into command form the passion eloquently found in the Psalms: "Whom have I in heaven but you? I desire you more than anything on earth" (Psalm 73:25). This is the deep and abiding desire he calls us to pursue.

STARVING FOR GOD

Scripture employs a variety of metaphors to drive home the intensity and the wonder of this desire. One set traffics in the idea of bodily nourishment—hunger and thirst.

We see this first in the Exodus account, where Moses explains one lesson from the miracle of manna: "He humbled you by letting you go hungry and then feeding you with manna, a food previously unknown to you and your ancestors. He did it to teach you that people do not live by bread alone; rather, we live by every word that comes from the mouth of the LORD" (Deuteronomy 8:3).

This, of course, is the verse Jesus quotes when tempted by Satan to break his fast. But this isn't the only time Jesus employs this metaphor. On another occasion, he explains to a crowd that his Father was responsible for feeding the

Israelites in the desert with bread from heaven, but he now offers "the true bread from heaven."

His listeners reply, "Give us that bread every day."

Jesus responds, "I am the bread of life. Whoever comes to me will never be hungry again. Whoever believes in me will never be thirsty" (John 6:32-35).

When his listeners become increasingly disturbed by this teaching, Jesus doubles down, saying something that no doubt startles them: "I tell you the truth, unless you eat the flesh of the Son of Man and drink his blood, you cannot have eternal life within you. . . . For my flesh is true food, and my blood is true drink. Anyone who eats my flesh and drinks my blood remains in me, and I in him" (verses 53-56).

It is a violent, frankly cannibalistic image meant to shock them into a deeper reality—the intense and personal nature of our union with God. Just as food and drink nourish and sustain us and become part of our bodies, so Jesus can sustain, nurture, and become one with us in spirit. And if we want such an intimate and life-sustaining union, we will hunger and thirst for it like nothing else.

I and many of my readers live in lands of abundance, so the biblical metaphor probably does not quite register. Our pangs of hunger needn't last but for a few minutes. Within ready reach—in a refrigerator or store or vending machine— is something to nourish us. Hunger for us is a mere inconvenience and food an entertainment. We watch reality TV shows that revel in the abundance of food and in the creativity of chefs, and some of us pride ourselves in being "foodies."

The biblical writers knew little of the affluence we enjoy.

It was not uncommon for them to endure periods of drought or famine. Food was neither a hobby nor about satisfying cravings but often a matter of life and death.

They would much more likely identify with the sufferers of modern-day famines. Christopher Hitchens describes one such famine he witnessed on a trip to North Korea:

> In the fields, you can see people picking up loose grains of rice and kernels of corn, gleaning every scrap. They look pinched and exhausted. In the few, dingy restaurants in the city, and even in the few modern hotels, you can read the *Pyongyang Times* through the soup, or the tea, or the coffee. Morsels of inexplicable fat or gristle are served as "duck." One evening I gave in and tried a bowl of dog stew, which at least tasted hearty and spicy . . . but then found my appetite crucially diminished by the realization that I hadn't seen a domestic animal, not even the merest cat, in the whole time I was there.[1]

To hunger and thirst for God in the biblical sense is to be desperate for God. The psalmist, among others, believes he is starved and dehydrated without God, as one whose skin sucks on his bones and exposes his skeleton, whose listlessness fuels his despair, who scours the ground for even a single grain of rice. The psalmist so desires to know God and his love—and here's where the nourishment metaphor is ironically transcended—that he says it is "better than life itself" (Psalm 63:3).

THE ROMANCE OF GOD

Romantic love is another biblical metaphor that pictures this desire.

In our age, we have recovered the original meaning of the Song of Solomon as a celebration of romantic love between a man and a woman. But for centuries, the church has also rightly understood romantic love as a symbol of the love between God and his people. For example, Bernard of Clairvaux published eighty-six sermons on the Song of Solomon, waxing eloquent on just this theme.

Bernard came by this interpretation honestly and biblically. Perhaps the most well-known use of the metaphor is found in the apostle Paul's discussion of marital love, saying that in some ways it pictures the love between God and us: "As the Scriptures say, 'A man leaves his father and mother and is joined to his wife, and the two are united into one.' This is a great mystery, but it is an illustration of the way Christ and the church are one" (Ephesians 5:31-32).

And he uses the metaphor elsewhere, as well: "For I am jealous for you with the jealousy of God himself. I promised you as a pure bride to one husband—Christ" (2 Corinthians 11:2).

Paul came by this metaphor honestly as well, drawing on the many Old Testament passages that pictured God as the bridegroom and Israel as the bride. Take this from the prophet Isaiah:

"Your Creator will be your husband;
the LORD of Heaven's Armies is his name!

He is your Redeemer, the Holy One of Israel,
    the God of all the earth.
For the LORD has called you back from your grief—
    as though you were a young wife abandoned by
      her husband,"
    says your God.

ISAIAH 54:5-6

Perhaps the most famous and extended use of the metaphor comes from Hosea:

I will make you my wife forever,
    showing you righteousness and justice,
    unfailing love and compassion.
I will be faithful to you and make you mine,
    and you will finally know me as the LORD.

HOSEA 2:19-20

Jesus picks up this theme, using wedding imagery in his parables to picture our relationship with God in the Kingdom of Heaven: "The Kingdom of Heaven can be illustrated by the story of a king who prepared a great wedding feast for his son" (Matthew 22:2).

And this (along with the nourishment metaphor) is carried through to the end of the Bible, in the vision of the culmination of all things:

"Praise the LORD!
    For the Lord our God, the Almighty, reigns.

Let us be glad and rejoice,
    and let us give honor to him.
For the time has come for the wedding feast of
    the Lamb,
    and his bride has prepared herself.
She has been given the finest of pure white linen
    to wear."
    For the fine linen represents the good deeds of
    God's holy people.

REVELATION 19:6-8

It is no wonder, then, that Bernard, among other church writers, exploits this metaphor as he opens his sermon series on the Song of Solomon. In sermon 3, in explaining the meaning of "Let him kiss me with the kiss of his mouth," he says,

Any one who has received this mystical kiss from
the mouth of Christ at least once, seeks again
that intimate experience, and eagerly looks for its
frequent renewal. I think that nobody can grasp
what it is except the one who receives it. For it is
"a hidden manna," and only he who eats it still
hungers for more.[2]

(Note how he employs the nourishment metaphor as well.)

In short, the desire for God is not unlike falling in love, in which the lovestruck desire nothing else but to be with the beloved. It's like the physical passion young lovers feel for each other. And it's like the ecstasy of sexual union that momentarily satisfies ever so deeply but before long grows into a desire to know ecstasy again.

PROTO-EVANGELICALS

Bernard is one of many proto-evangelicals in his emphasis on the personal, intimate, and passionate relationship we can have with God. As he put it in *On Loving God*,

> He is all that I need, all that I long for. My God and my help, I will love Thee for Thy great goodness; not so much as I might, surely, but as much as I can. I cannot love Thee as Thou deservest to be loved, for I cannot love Thee more than my own feebleness permits. I will love Thee more when Thou deemest me worthy to receive greater capacity for loving; yet never so perfectly as Thou hast deserved of me.[3]

To encounter the living God is to meet with two realities at the same time. The first was expressed no more eloquently than by the philosopher and mathematician Blaise Pascal, when he haltingly described, seemingly while it was happening, his stunning vision:

THE YEAR OF GRACE 1654, MONDAY, 23 NOVEMBER

From about half past ten at night until about half past midnight—

22

FIRE.
GOD of Abraham, GOD of Isaac, GOD of Jacob
   not of the philosophers and of the learned.
Certitude. Certitude. Feeling. Joy. Peace.
GOD of Jesus Christ.
My God and your God.
Your GOD will be my God.
Forgetfulness of the world and of everything,
   except GOD.[4]

Many a saint has experienced this reality, if not in a direct, overwhelming vision, certainly in some encounter they can never shake. They can never shake it because of the second reality that accompanies an encounter with the living God— its insatiableness. C. S. Lewis talked about such an experience as an encounter with joy:

> It is difficult to find words strong enough for
> the sensation which came over me. . . . It was
> a sensation, of course, of desire; but desire for
> what? . . . An unsatisfied desire which is itself
> more desirable than any other satisfaction. I call
> it Joy, which is here a technical term and must be
> sharply distinguished both from Happiness and
> from Pleasure. Joy (in my sense) has indeed one
> characteristic, and one only, in common with
> them; the fact that anyone who has experienced
> it will want it again.[5]

The cardinal mistake in some Christian circles is telling people that knowing God will bring us peace. Yes, in the sense of knowing forgiveness and purpose in life. But in a deeper sense, an encounter with God brings us not only satisfaction but also deep dissatisfaction, not just fulfillment but also longing, and a longing that can never be fulfilled. In her *Revelations of Divine Love*, Julian of Norwich called it "an unbearable desire." She wrote, "If he graciously lets us see something of himself, then we are moved by the same grace to seek with a great longing to see him more fully." She put it best when she said, "I saw him and I sought him, I had him and I wanted him."[6]

We are longing for the infinite, for that to which all other desires only point. And when our desires are fulfilled however briefly, we recognize how much more there is in God's beauty and wonder and love. We can never exhaust God's wonder and glory—and for that very reason it is the most precious of longings.

Again, a person like me is tempted to say that longing is given only to a few naturally spiritual people. They have a unique desire for God, but most of us desire concrete realities and have special passions for, perhaps, food and drink, or romance and love, or fine music or fine art, or to be in the splendor of creation, and so forth. To each their own. This spiritual passion isn't for everybody, I think.

And yet Jesus says it is, in that he commands that we all pursue the love of God and pursue it to the fullest extent. This, like all commands, is not as much a "should" as it is a promise: do this, and you shall live. *Really* live.

In our restlessness, we flit from one thing to another as we follow our desires, hoping against hope to find something, anything, that will cure our boredom and satisfy our longings. Everything we pursue—financial security, love, fulfillment in a calling, the joy of a hobby or pastime, and so forth—are mere pointers to something more true, more good, and more beautiful. We remain restless precisely because we mistake these shadows for the real thing.

At our worst, we make idols out of the penultimate things we desire. At our most innocent, we are like confused travelers who rejoice in reaching a milestone as if we've arrived at our glorious destination. In either case, there is something better that awaits us. Augustine, in reflecting on his youth, said, "I sought pleasure, nobility, and truth not in God but in the beings He had created, myself and others. Thus I fell into sorrow and confusion and error. Thanks be to Thee, my Joy and my Glory and my Hope and my God: thanks be to Thee for Thy gifts."[7]

In commenting on this, Augustine scholar Michael Foley has noted that this passage outlines Augustine's theology of desire: "The appetite for physical pleasure is ultimately a groaning for happiness in God, and thus the attempt to satisfy it with created goods instead of the Creator ends in sorrow rather than joy."[8] The same applies to the yearning for nobility and truth.

Thus there is no one who is not "into God," so to speak. The only thing at issue is whether we are aware of what our desires are for and where they are designed to lead us. As

Augustine famously and succinctly put it, "Our hearts are restless until they find their rest in thee."

To desire God—this is the sum and substance of life. It's not just one injunction of many, but the *greatest* commandment. It's not merely a duty to fulfill but the fulfillment of life itself—to love God with all our heart, all our soul, all our mind, and all our strength. There is no greater blessing than to give oneself to this pursuit and to enjoy the everlasting longing it produces in us. This is what the Westminster Shorter Catechism is getting at when it says that the chief purpose of men and women is "to glorify God, and to enjoy him forever."

So the psalmist is not neurotic or an emotional wreck, as I am sometimes tempted to think, but the sanest of human creatures. If this monomania is a mental illness, then let us all share in it. The church is not only a hospital for sinners but also an asylum for those disturbed saints who are monomaniacs for God, who want nothing but to seek after him, knowing full well that the pursuit will never end, and yet knowing too that there is nothing better to do with one's life: "I saw him and I sought him, I had him and I wanted him."

CHAPTER 2

WE HAVE FORGOTTEN GOD

THE LONGING TO KNOW and love God, to bask in his presence, is core to evangelical life and faith as I understand it. The famous Bebbington quadrilateral describes evangelicals as those who emphasize the need for conversion, a life of service in both word and deed, the authority of Scripture, and Christ's death on the cross. That is good as far as it goes, but it does not go deep enough, in my view. There is something that initiates our first and sustains our ongoing conversion, that energizes our action, that compels us to read and obey Scripture, that draws us repeatedly to the Cross. That *something* is the yearning to know God.

One can still find this yearning in our movement today, but it is no longer something that *characterizes* us. One reason

I believe the desire for God is core to what it means to be evangelical is what happened at our movement's birth, when the desire for God did indeed characterize us.

The following historical survey is woefully inadequate to prove this and the subsequent decline of our desire. But I nonetheless believe that, in broad strokes, it is a fair summary of where we've been and where we are today.

"THE TOWN SEEMED TO BE FULL OF THE PRESENCE OF GOD"

The American evangelical movement sprang up in the 1730s and 1740s when George Whitefield and John Wesley began preaching about the need to be born again. Their preaching revived a dying portion of Jesus' church, which reanimated a people so that they might enjoy a vital, living, and loving relationship with our Savior. The movement, known as the Great Awakening, blossomed as the message and experience of being born again spread, but often painfully as the larger body of Christ resisted the movement. But nothing could stop what was happening. Before long, there stood a movement of men and women, boys and girls, who—as they put it—had been washed clean of their sin by the blood of the Lamb. They cried out with the joy of being alive—really alive—for the first time. And they praised our Savior and loved him more than anything, more than life itself.

The theologian Jonathan Edwards did his best to describe what he saw happening around him:

This work of God, as it was carried on, and the number of true saints multiplied, soon made a glorious alteration in the town: so that in the spring and summer following, anno 1735, the town seemed to be full of the presence of God: it never was so full of love, nor of joy, and yet so full of distress, as it was then. There were remarkable tokens of God's presence in almost every house. It was a time of joy in families on account of salvation being brought unto them; parents rejoicing over their children as new born, and husbands over their wives, and wives over their husbands. The goings of God were then seen in his sanctuary, God's day was a delight, and his tabernacles were amiable. . . .

In all companies, on other days, on whatever occasions persons met together, Christ was to be heard of, and seen in the midst of them. Our young people, when they met, were wont to spend the time in talking of the excellency and dying love of Jesus Christ, the glory of the way of salvation, the wonderful, free, and sovereign grace of God, his glorious work in the conversion of a soul, the truth and certainty of the great things of God's word, the sweetness of the views of his perfections.[1]

Evangelical faith soon became characterized by a lively, personal relationship with God, grounded in the death and resurrection of Jesus Christ, with a deep and abiding trust in the Bible as God's personal Word to us, and with an active desire to spread this gospel to others. These emphases—especially that lively and personal relationship with God—can be seen in many eras of church history, and in this sense evangelical religion goes back to the beginnings of the Christian faith. But its modern, American form finds its birth here, in a season when whole towns "seemed to be full of the presence of God."

After the Revolutionary War, as the exhausted nation moved west in the late 1700s, enthusiasm—*en theos*, the yearning to be in God and to know God in us—was replaced by other concerns. On a trip to Tennessee in 1797, Methodist bishop Francis Asbury noted, "When I reflect that not one in a hundred came here to get religion, but rather to get plenty of good land, I think it will be well if some or many do not eventually lose their souls." Andrew Fulton, a Presbyterian missionary from Scotland, observed anxiously that in "all the newly formed towns in this western colony [around Nashville, Tennessee], there are few religious people." Others worried that many Christians had become universalists and deists, the latter especially asserting God's distance from this world.

Still, there were some who, at the first sign of a flagging spirit, prayed for God to make himself known again. They prayed at home, in their churches, at denominational meetings, and at retreats that would climax in the sharing of the Lord's Supper. And their prayers were answered at Cane Ridge, Kentucky, in 1801, when some twenty thousand showed up to be touched by the Spirit of God.

Their enthusiasm for God spread into what is now called

the Second Great Awakening. It eventually found expression in circuit riders and Methodist camp meetings and periodic revival meetings of local churches. One observer at a small revival previous to Cane Ridge described what was to happen to so many in the years to come: "No person seemed to wish to go home—hunger and sleep seemed to affect nobody— eternal things were the vast concern."[2]

FROM THE SUBLIME TO TECHNIQUE

Historians have noted that these revivals were in some ways a reaction against Enlightenment rationality, which often marshaled reason and science to question and marginalize religion. The larger reaction—Romanticism—encompassed the arts, literature, music, and philosophy, which together exalted the role of intuition and emotion in human affairs. Many Christians expressed their disdain for Enlightenment values by praising revivals and noting that they could not be explained rationally but only spiritually as products of divine intervention.

But some Christians, already deeply influenced by the Enlightenment, looked at these revivals rationally and noticed sociological patterns. And they began applying them to their ministries. The most famous is Charles Finney. In his *Lectures on Revivals of Religion*, he argued that a revival was "not a miracle, or dependent on a miracle, in any sense. It is a purely philosophical [meaning scientific] result of the right use of constituted means."[3] To be sure, he believed God gave these means to produce revivals, but as Tim Keller puts it, "Finney insisted that any group could have a revival any time or place, as long as they applied the right methods in the right way."[4]

This philosophy of revival morphed into a religion of crisis, a religion of decision, and a religion where the manipulation of emotion became the centerpiece. Instead of being characterized by a genuine encounter with the living God, the movement became infected with too many who sought not so much to know and love God as to have a remarkable religious experience. This has been our Achilles' heel ever since.

Some were alert to this corruption early on and reacted against it. One reason: try as they might, this genuine religious ecstasy never came to them. One such person, Phoebe Palmer, after a crisis of faith, determined that "she didn't need 'joyous emotion' to believe—belief itself was grounds for assurance. Reading Jesus' words that 'the altar sanctifies the gift,' she believed that God would make her holy if she 'laid her all upon the altar.'" Palmer fine-tuned John Wesley's teachings about perfectionism "into a three-step process: consecrating oneself totally to God, believing God will sanctify what is consecrated, and telling others about it."[5]

Out of this grew the holiness movement, where complete sanctification stood at the center. The life of faith became not so much pining after God but pining after moral perfection, not so much seeking grace as pummeling the will into submission. No question that there was a need to depend on the power of the Spirit, and many in this movement rigorously pursued holiness that they might see God: the holiness movement produced more than its share of Protestant saints. But much of it also predictably degenerated into religious narcissism. For many, it was more and more about the pursuit of personal holiness than the pursuit of the Holy One.

This passion for personal reform soon spilled over into the social realm so that evangelical believers also became known for striving for the reformation of society—from prison reform to abstinence to the abolition of slavery to care for the urban poor. And for some, this blossomed into the social gospel movement, whose gospel origins and godly motives one cannot deny.

Walter Rauschenbusch in his *A Theology for the Social Gospel* said, "The new thing in the social gospel is the clearness and insistence with which it sets forth the necessity and the possibility of redeeming the historical life of humanity from the social wrongs which now pervade it."[6] Though evangelicals today reject Rauschenbusch's theological liberalism, his emphasis on the church's mission has woven itself into the very fabric of evangelical religion. Mission, and all the activity surrounding it, has become the very reason for the church's existence. More on that in the coming chapters.

It must be said that such activity for God is laudatory. One of the jobs of the church is indeed to love the world. But when mission becomes the focal point of the Christian life, I believe that life will inevitably degenerate into an active and busy religious life void of God. It will become a life fascinated with technique and method as it seeks to efficiently accomplish its mission. We may begin and end our missional meetings with prayer, but we know deep down that we don't need God's special blessing if, as Finney argued, we already have the means at our disposal to accomplish our ends.

FROM GOD TO SPIRITUAL EXPERIENCE

In the midst of this drift toward action, another movement arose, a kind of new spiritual romanticism that tried to check our fascination with the horizontal and reengage us with the vertical. The Pentecostal movement exploded on the scene at the turn of the twentieth century, beginning with a revival at Azusa Street in Los Angeles, which can be characterized, among other manifestations, like this:

> There were no hymnals, no liturgy, no order of
> services. Most of the time there were no musical
> instruments. But around the room, men jumped
> and shouted. Women danced and sang. People sang
> sometimes together, yet with completely different
> syllables, rhythms, and melodies. At other times
> the church joined together in English versions
> of "The Comforter Has Come," "Fill Me Now,"
> "Joy Unspeakable," and "Love Lifted Me."[7]

More than anything, people experienced an immediate sense of being filled with the Holy Spirit, which was manifested especially in the gift of tongues. Though questioned by a skeptical mainstream church, a milder version of this revival—charismatic Christianity—eventually made its way into their pews beginning in April 1960, when Dennis Bennett, rector of St. Mark's Episcopal Church in Van Nuys, California, announced to his congregation that he had experienced the gift of tongues.[8]

As with many revival movements, controversy erupts when people are moved by the Spirit, with charges of extremism on the one hand and doctrinal division on the other. But overall, men and women influenced by these movements enjoyed the immediate presence of God as he came to them in the Holy Spirit. And so people came to these meetings in droves because they yearned for God.

But with this yearning comes a subtle yet real temptation: the yearning for God can turn into a longing for a certain type of spiritual experience. Instead of God, people begin wanting to experience the extraordinary gifts of God—and leaders sometimes manipulate congregations in this direction. For many Pentecostals, tongues became not so much a means of conversing with the living God as much as a sign or a proof of one's spiritual condition—that is, "evidence of receiving the baptism [of the Holy Spirit]."[9]

This is not throwing stones. Believe me, as someone who has been blessed with some of the more charismatic spiritual gifts, I too have longed for more and more spiritual experiences for their own sake—and truth be told, I wanted these experiences more than I wanted God. Most people who have experienced such extraordinary gifts know the temptation here.

FROM HOLINESS TO TRANSFORMATION

Transformation has become a popular topic in evangelical churches. A few years ago, a church I attended asked me if I would stand before the congregation with others, each of us wearing a sign that said "Transformed." We were then to give a one- or two-sentence summary about how God had transformed some aspect of our lives. At the time, I refused because I thought it prideful to stand before others claiming I had been transformed. I thought if I had been transformed in some way, others would notice, and if they didn't, I didn't want to be bragging about it!

A few years later I figured out what had bothered me. I see how the idea of *transformation* has increasingly filled the air of evangelical churches. As I wrote a decade ago, "Transformation is the evangelical mantra of our times. Everyone either hopes for it or promises it. Transformation of self. Transformation of church. Transformation of culture."[10]

Once again, one cannot help but be impressed by the efforts of evangelicals left, right, and center to transform everything from the self to the culture. Better this than sitting in our easy chairs reading books about evangelicals forgetting God! But as with every other thing we touch, we are sorely tempted not only to focus on the horizontal but also to use the vertical to accomplish the horizontal, meaning we have a tendency to think that what we do in our lives and in our world is more important than knowing God.

I have seen this temptation express itself subtly but plainly whenever I have suggested that transformation may not be all it's cracked up to be. Progress, after all, can be so slow and halting that a great saint like the apostle Paul, who wrote, "Forgetting the past and looking forward to what lies ahead, I press on to reach the end of the race and receive the heavenly prize for which God, through Christ Jesus, is calling us" (Philippians 3:13-14), still calls himself at the end of his

life "the worst" of sinners (see 1 Timothy 1:15). To which
the response is often, "What's the point of being a Christian
if it's not going to make a difference?" When I hear that, it
suggests to me that the person may be a Christian mainly
because they are tired of who they are, weary with the self
that has accompanied them their whole lives, and now more
than anything they want to be changed. And so they come
to God, believing that he can change those aspects of themselves they find disgusting.

Can you see what's happening here? In our desire for
transformation, God is a means to an end. That's not love of
God. That's love of self.

It's my impression that much of the talk about transformation in evangelicalism is more interested in transformation than in God, or interested in God mostly because of
how he can change people's lives, families, and communities.

We hear the same sort of connection in social justice
circles. Pursuing justice for the unborn or the immigrant
or the victim of racial prejudice and so on—it's exhausting
work. Admirable work, but exhausting. And within a few
years, if not a few months, most Christians engaged in such
work find they need to spend more time in the Bible and in
prayer, and this is the way they often put it: "I will not be
able to sustain a commitment to justice if I'm not regularly
engaged in prayer and biblical meditation." This is as true as
true can be. But can we see what has happened here? God
becomes a means to the justice workers' end—perseverance
in the work.

A more insidious temptation around transformation in

social justice has been critical theory, in which power dynamics are front and center, especially in race and gender relations. Just as with early Marxism every social situation was analyzed in terms of class, today (depending on the topic) everything is analyzed in terms of race or gender dynamics. It's a purely horizontal way of trying to grasp a social situation, with no or little reference to vertical factors like the providence of God or redemptive suffering in Christ or a dozen other theological insights that can be brought to bear on a social injustice.

On the other end of the political spectrum, we have the unsightly appearance of seemingly devout evangelicals defending or simply ignoring a chief executive's blatantly immoral behavior and speech. Donald Trump is clearly the most immoral president in the history of the United States, but there are some evangelicals who pretend like that's not important. Why?

Because they are fearful that simply acknowledging this, let alone speaking out against the president's behavior, might undermine his power. And why is that a problem? Because devotion to the horizontal—the health of the nation as they see it—has blinded them to the obligations owed to God, one of which is addressing evil behavior in our leaders (as did John the Baptist against the "president" of his time, at the cost of his life—see Matthew 14:1-12). I'm not talking about evangelicals who voted for Mr. Trump while holding their noses, who readily acknowledge the ever-persistent immoralities of the president but viewed him as the better option given the choices. There is an entire group of self-identifying evangelicals who have apparently sold their souls to a political end in the name of transformation in their nation.

Another area where transformation has run amok is in the megachurch. The idea of the megachurch is hardly a problem in itself: there have always been large churches in the history of Christianity. But we live in an impatient time when we look less for pastors who can faithfully preach the Word and more for entrepreneurs who can plant and build churches. After all, if your goal is to transform the world, you must first transform your community, and that begins by either planting or transforming your church into something that can make a difference in the world.

We have failed to take into account the cost of this whole enterprise, and the cost is seen in the ambition of many megachurch pastors, which often manifests itself in abuses of power, manipulation of church funds, a loneliness that seeks out extramarital release, alcoholism, and depression. At *Christianity Today*, we've reported on too many situations like this, and more and more come our way every month. Some of this is due to the weakness of human nature, but a lot of it has to do with our passion for church and community transformation above all else and what that requires of a modern pastor.

One cannot but be thankful for our passion for transformation in all spheres of life. Christians whose hearts don't sink at the sinfulness of their lives or the spiritual needs of their communities or the injustices that infect every society—well, it's hard to believe they can truly love the God of the

Bible. But the enemy has a way of twisting our good passions so that we slowly forget God in pursuit of them.

THE SUM OF THE PROBLEM

A friend's experience drives home the essential nature of our faith today and our tendency to forget God.

This friend has been striving to make God his be-all and end-all, one for whom he pants as a deer after water. So he had given himself to praying during certain hours of the day, especially morning and at bedtime, and if possible once or twice in the middle of his busy days. The prayer time included praying the Psalms and reading other Scripture, as well as quiet meditation on the Word. All of this lasted no more than ten to fifteen minutes, but he found it is a practice he enjoys, not in the sense of checking off a box but in the sense that he is slowly but surely finding his love for God growing.

But his heart remains confused. One day recently he left work early to attend to some tasks and to play golf. On the way home, he determined to have a prayer time before he changed and left to do these tasks and to play. He found himself in the car thirty minutes later, having completely forgotten about his intent to pray.

Why was he so intent on getting these tasks done that they consumed his mind? he wondered. What was it about this recreational activity that so captured his imagination that he couldn't forget doing it, while it was so easy to forget to pray?

And why was it, he also wondered, that many mornings he noted a reluctance in his heart to sit down to pray, especially when there were so many things on his to-do list? Why didn't he consider prayer one of these absolutely necessary things to do, and why didn't he look forward to it if, in fact, God is the source of all life and joy and the deepest satisfaction of our deepest desires? If he loved and desired God, as he said he wanted to, why did the loves and desires of so much else actually shape his day and his heart?

He concluded, "When it comes down to it, I'm a practical atheist. I've learned to live most of my life as if God is a nice add-on—when I have time and when I really want him—but otherwise I'm content with living as if he is not a living presence."

As I noted in the introduction, I deeply identify with my friend's dilemma.[11] And in talking with many friends, I'd say we're not alone. So it's not quite true that we've completely forgotten God. But our spiritual Alzheimer's has progressed to dangerous levels.

This is a very common human condition. It is not remarkably evil that we are so distracted by life and responsibilities and earthly desires that God takes a decided back seat. We needn't whip ourselves with guilt over this. This chapter and the book are not a wholesale condemnation but a wake-up call that there is something better that awaits us.

I think it is especially incumbent on evangelical Christians to treat this situation with special seriousness. We have rightly prided ourselves in practicing a form of faith that emphasizes a personal relationship with Jesus. One can argue, as I have in this chapter, that this is at the heart of what it means to be evangelical—to know, love, and obey Jesus as if he were a friend, as if he "walks with us and talks with us along life's narrow way," as the old hymn put it. If there is to be an evangelical Christianity with the vitality to survive and thrive in the coming decades, I believe the born-again movement must be born again *again* into a living, vital, and personal relationship with God, a relationship that floods our hearts and minds as it did for the psalmists and so many others in the Bible and in our history.

The journey back to God, so to speak, begins inside the church. So crucial is the church that the entire next section is devoted to how we think about and live in the church. Our relentless horizontal focus has penetrated the everyday life of the church, from worship to preaching to small groups. But before we go there, I will start by suggesting that the way we think about the church needs to be grounded in a completely different way.

PART 2

THE
CHURCH

CHAPTER 3

RETHINKING THE CHURCH: THE PROBLEM WITH A MISSIONAL MIND-SET

THERE IS NO BETTER PLACE to begin thinking more deeply about how the horizontal has eclipsed the vertical—and how we can reimagine the vertical—than to think about the church. Thus in this section, I want to address our very theology of church, as well as how various aspects of church life can better support the vertical.

Evangelical faith is often criticized for having no ecclesiology—that is, no doctrine of the church. I beg to differ and instead say that it has an inadequate and truncated doctrine of the church. It's one reason I believe the movement is in crisis.

A few years ago, I was interviewing Rob Bell for *Christianity Today* about his book *Jesus Wants to Save Christians*. He had written something in the book that surprised me, so I asked him to clarify himself: "What to you is the purpose of the church?"

"The purpose of the church," he replied, "is to make the world a better place." That's what he had said in the book, and that's the statement that puzzled me. I frankly couldn't believe he had said that in front of God and everybody. But as I thought about it, I realized that Bell had expressed precisely the current zeitgeist of the American church. I was less concerned about Bell than I was about the church.

Some background might explain what concerned me.

FROM SOCIAL GOSPEL TO MISSIONAL

From the midsixties until 1989, I was a member and then a minister in what is now called PC(USA), the mainline Presbyterian church. For the next fourteen years, I was a member of the Episcopal Church. For over four decades, I had been embedded in mainline/liberal Christianity. And most in this tradition assume that the church's purpose is to make the world a better place. This view is not held by everyone, everywhere in the mainline, nor is it always said in just this way. But it is clearly a widespread assumption.

This purpose was born in the late nineteenth and early twentieth centuries. It was articulated most cogently by Baptist theologian and activist Walter Rauschenbusch in his *A Theology for the Social Gospel*.[1] In it he said, "The new thing in the social gospel is the clearness and insistence with which it sets forth the necessity and the possibility of redeeming the historical life of humanity from the social wrongs which now pervade it."[2]

Rauschenbusch was driven to this conclusion by his conception of the Kingdom of God. While acknowledging the need for individual salvation, he was most concerned about social salvation—thus the *social* gospel. "To those whose minds live in the social gospel," he said, "the Kingdom of God is a dear truth, the marrow of the gospel, just as the incarnation was to Athanasius, justification by faith alone to Luther, and the sovereignty of God to Jonathan Edwards."[3]

Therefore, he said later, "Since the Kingdom is the supreme end of God, it must be the purpose for which the Church exists. . . . The institutions of the Church, its activities, its worship, and its theology must in the long run be tested by its effectiveness in creating the Kingdom of God."[4]

Rauschenbusch believed that the Kingdom of God/social gospel was the concept that could reinvigorate a dead church: "If the Kingdom had stood as the purpose for which the Church exists, the Church could not have fallen into such corruption and sloth."[5] In addition, he contended that this concept elevates the church: "Within the field it has chosen to cultivate, the local church under good leadership is really a power of salvation."[6] But lest the church take itself too seriously, he also noted, "The Kingdom of God is not confined within the limits of the Church and its activities. It embraces the whole of human life. It is the Christian transfiguration of the social order. The Church is one social institution alongside of the family, the industrial organization of society, and the State."[7]

In other words, the purpose of the church—like all other social institutions—is to make the world a better place. Or to put it another way, the church exists for the sake of the world.

Rauschenbusch's theology, and the entire optimistic liberal project, was seemingly discredited by the disasters called World War I and World War II and the incisive and bold critiques of neoorthodox theologians. But it has since been making a comeback. It may have started, ironically enough, with the neoorthodox Emil Brunner, who in *The Word and the World* said, "The church exists by mission, just as a fire exists by burning."[8] In other words, the church's very lifeblood is its work in the world.

At the end of the last century, the great church statesman and missionary theologian Lesslie Newbigin reinvigorated the missionary purpose of the church. Newbigin has had a deep influence on contemporary evangelicalism, and his thought is nuanced and careful. But missiologist Wilbert Shenk's summary of Newbigin is what many of his readers have taken away:

> We are being called to reclaim the church for its
> missionary purpose. . . . Mission is often treated as
> a stepchild or, even worse, in some cases an orphan.
> That is to say, traditional ecclesiology has had no
> place for mission. Yet the church was instituted
> by Jesus Christ to be a sign of God's reign and
> the means of witnessing to that reign throughout
> the world. The church that refuses to accept its
> missionary purpose is a deformed church. . . .

We are being called to reclaim the church for its missionary purpose in relation to modern Western culture.[9]

As I noted, Newbigin's theology is larger than this, but this is what has made a great impact on evangelical leaders. Perhaps the prime example is what's called the missional movement. As with most movements, the very term itself is in dispute and comes to us in many colors. It is often combined with a fresh appreciation of Kingdom theology, an attempt to let Jesus' preaching about the Kingdom of God become the hub of the wheel of our theology. Many missional advocates see this as not *their* mission but as the mission of God, which they are merely joining. We needn't deny the many flavors of missional, or its obvious strengths, to grasp that for many pastors and theologians, the purpose of the church can be summarized like this (from a church blog I happened upon):

> After Jesus was resurrected and after he had spent significant time schooling the nascent church, as He Himself had been sent, He sent His church on a mission, and sent the Holy Spirit to empower them for that task until the end of time, to the very ends of the earth. As Jesus was sent, and as the Spirit was sent, in like manner, the church has been sent. Therefore, the church exists missionally, sent by the triune God to carry out the mission of making disciples of all nations. Wherever the church exists,

it exists for the sake of the world, as a sign and proclamation of the kingdom of God.[10]

The most incisive and thorough apology for the missional church is Christopher Wright's *The Mission of God: Unlocking the Bible's Grand Narrative*. It is a great book, with a deep and nuanced theological grounding. It is widely read and quoted in the missional community, and for good reason. I hesitate to critique it because it has so much valuable thinking for us to ponder. But Wright's fundamental understanding of the Bible is, in my view, problematic. He writes, "Mission is what the Bible is all about,"[11] and earlier in the book, he defines what mission is: "I will use the term *mission* in its general sense of a long-term purpose or goal that is to be achieved through proximate objectives and planned actions."[12]

As I hope to show in the chapters that follow, I believe that *God* is what the Bible is all about. Wright has some fine chapters on the God who makes himself known to Israel and then to the world in Jesus Christ. It seems to me, though, that the Bible is about God first and foremost and that making him known is crucial but in fact secondary. The main theological problem with imagining that God has a mission to make himself known is that, after achieving his "long-term purpose . . . achieved through proximate objectives" (the Kingdom of Heaven), God will have nothing to do, or will have to change his nature and purpose. The "mission of God" perspective tempts us to create a god in our image, one who is restlessly working to achieve some end, one who feeds our addiction to activity.

I have no quarrel with activity or mission—you can't be the church of Jesus Christ and not seek to love your neighbor in all sorts of ways. But for all its inspirational value—and this is not to be denied or denigrated—in the end, missional thinking tends to reduce the purpose of the church in the same way as Rauschenbusch does: "Wherever the church exists, it exists for the sake of the world."

The careful reader will have suspected my point in rehearsing all this: I think this view is mistaken, and mistaken on two grounds. I believe it is an unbiblical view of the church. And I believe it is an unhealthy diet for the church. Why? Ultimately because it only encourages our addiction to activity and makes it ever harder for us to want to seek God.

CHAPTER 4

RETHINKING THE CHURCH: A BIBLICAL PICTURE

To GRASP THE FIRST POINT—that our view of church is unbiblical—I begin by looking at Paul's letter to the Ephesians. Let me acknowledge that what follows is not a formal ecclesiology, which would require book-length treatment and a fair amount of interaction with other theologians. Instead, this is a call to ask us to think again about how we view the church.

While Ephesians is not a systematic theology of the church, it is where Paul outlines most deeply and consistently a theology of the church. Paul begins his letter with hardly any warm-up. He jumps in by outlining a breathtaking view of history, in which the role of the church is central:

Blessed be the God and Father of our Lord Jesus Christ, who has blessed us in Christ with every spiritual blessing in the heavenly places, just as he chose us in Christ before the foundation of the world to be holy and blameless before him in love. He destined us for adoption as his children through Jesus Christ, according to the good pleasure of his will, to the praise of his glorious grace that he freely bestowed on us in the Beloved. In him we have redemption through his blood, the forgiveness of our trespasses, according to the riches of his grace that he lavished on us. With all wisdom and insight he has made known to us the mystery of his will, according to his good pleasure that he set forth in Christ, as a plan for the fullness of time, to gather up all things in him, things in heaven and things on earth.

EPHESIANS 1:3-10, NRSV

The most important thing to note is Paul's understanding of the mind of God before the creation of the world: "Before the foundation of the world," he says, God's first and primary purpose was to create a people for himself, who would live with him "holy and blameless before him in love." Before and above anything else, he thought about a people he would adopt as family, who would be brothers and sisters of Jesus his Son.

He did this not for some ulterior motive, so that this family would then go out and do something even more important. He did this "according to the good pleasure of his will" and "to the praise of his glorious grace"—meaning because of the simple splendidness of the act. It appears that for Paul, the family of God—the church—is not a means but an end.

The church is in fact the sign and portent of God's universal will, which is "a plan for the fullness of time, to gather up all things in him, things in heaven and things on earth." God's wish is to bring everything into his orbit of love. The plan seems to be this: everywhere, as far as the eye can see, there will be the family of God—the church—living before their Father in holy love.

Paul continues: "In Christ we have also obtained an inheritance, having been destined according to the purpose of him who accomplishes all things according to his counsel and will, so that we, who were the first to set our hope on Christ, might live for the praise of his glory" (Ephesians 1:11-12, NRSV).

Notice how Paul talks about what we do in light of our being called into the church. Given our interest in things missional, we might expect to read, "We have obtained this inheritance, we have been destined according to God's will, so that we, who were first to set our hope in Christ, might live to share that hope with those who don't know hope."

Or "We, who were first to set our hope in Christ, might live to further the Kingdom of God in the world."

Or "We, who were the first to set our hope in Christ, might live to make the world a better place and foster human flourishing."

No. Paul's view of the church is not instrumentalist at all. Instead, he says that since we have been gathered into the church, we who have first set our hope in Christ should live praising God's glory.

The point is this: the church is its own end. It is created by God's good pleasure and for our good pleasure. As a result of being called into the family called church, our job is to bask in its sheer goodness by living together in holy love and by together praising God's glory for doing such a wonderful thing.

According to this summary passage, it does not appear that the church was created for the world. If anything, the world was created for the sake of the church. That is, the funnel of history is not that the church pours itself into the world to redeem it but that the world—at least those in the world who trust in Christ—is poured into the church.

Paul is not foisting a new idea on the Ephesians. His theology is grounded in the Old Testament. There we repeatedly read how Israel has been chosen by God and esteemed by God, created by God so he might have a people for himself.

One typical example is when the Lord speaks through Isaiah:

> But as for you, Israel my servant,
>   Jacob my chosen one,
>   descended from Abraham my friend,
> I have called you back from the ends of
>   the earth,
>   saying, "You are my servant."
> For I have chosen you
>   and will not throw you away.

ISAIAH 41:8-9

Abraham was called from the ends of the earth to be the father of God's chosen people, but also the people he fathers (by God's grace) become a sign of history's goal:

> In the last days, the mountain of the LORD's house
>   will be the highest of all—
>   the most important place on earth.
> It will be raised above the other hills,
>   and people from all over the world will stream
>   there to worship.
> People from many nations will come and say,
> "Come, let us go up to the mountain of the LORD,
>   to the house of Jacob's God.
> There he will teach us his ways,
>   and we will walk in his paths."

ISAIAH 2:2-3

In other words, the world comes to Jerusalem. Israel does not go out to the world missionally to transform the world, but at the end of history, the world comes to Mount Zion to worship and learn from God.

This image is repeated in the New Testament. In Revelation we read about a new Jerusalem coming down out of heaven, about which John says, "I saw no temple in the city, for the Lord God Almighty and the Lamb are its temple. And the city has no need of sun or moon, for the glory of God illuminates the city, and the Lamb is its light. The nations will walk in its light, and the kings of the world will enter the city in all their glory" (21:22-24).

Again, the image is that in the end, the world comes to the church, the place where people bask in the presence of God, where the pleasure of God is our pleasure, prompting us to erupt in praise: "No longer will there be a curse upon anything. For the throne of God and of the Lamb will be there, and his servants will worship him" (Revelation 22:3).

A vivid description of that worship is found earlier:

Whenever the living beings give glory and honor and thanks to the one sitting on the throne (the one who lives forever and ever), the twenty-four elders fall down and worship the one sitting on the throne (the one who lives forever and ever). And they lay their crowns before the throne and say,

"You are worthy, O Lord our God,
    to receive glory and honor and power.
For you created all things,
    and they exist because you created what
        you pleased."

REVELATION 4:9-11

My reading of the sweep of the biblical picture, then, is that the purpose of the church—the family of God—is not to make the world a better place but to invite the world *into* the better place, the church.

THE OTHER SIDE

I recognize this point of view is not widely held among evangelical Christians. Many verses in Scripture seem to suggest just the opposite—that the church is not an end but a means, that it was created for the sake of the world. So we need to look at some of these passages too.

The classic expression comes from Isaiah 42:

I, the LORD, have called you to demonstrate my
     righteousness.
   I will take you by the hand and guard you,
and I will give you to my people, Israel,
     as a symbol of my covenant with them.
And you will be a light to guide the nations.
   You will open the eyes of the blind.
You will free the captives from prison,
     releasing those who sit in dark dungeons.

ISAIAH 42:6-7

And let me be fair with my quote of Isaiah's vision, in which people from all over the globe come to Jerusalem. It ends like this: "For the LORD's teaching will go out from Zion; his word will go out from Jerusalem" (2:3).

And then there is this key statement of God to Abraham: "All the families on earth will be blessed through you" (Genesis 12:3).

Such verses are often used to suggest, among other things, that Israel failed in its primary mission—being a light to the

world—and that Jesus, at the end of his ministry, made sure
that the church was absolutely clear about its purpose:

> Then the eleven disciples left for Galilee, going to
> the mountain where Jesus had told them to go.
> When they saw him, they worshiped him—but
> some of them doubted!
>   Jesus came and told his disciples, "I have
> been given all authority in heaven and on earth.
> Therefore, go and make disciples of all the nations,
> baptizing them in the name of the Father and the
> Son and the Holy Spirit. Teach these new disciples
> to obey all the commands I have given you. And be
> sure of this: I am with you always, even to the end
> of the age."
> MATTHEW 28:16-20

What could be more clear? Such passages suggest that the
purpose of the church is to go out to all nations, to go out
into the world on mission, to be missional.

Not quite, in my view.

First, note the context of that key verse in Genesis. God
tells Abraham that his family will become a great nation and
that those who bless this great nation will be blessed and
those who curse this nation will be cursed. The implication
is that all the other families of the earth will be blessed as they
bless the family of Abraham. It's not about Abraham's missionary purpose but about the status of Abraham's family in
the eyes of the world. The nation of Israel is a sign of God's

ultimate purpose—to create a people for himself—and those who recognize and honor that will be blessed.

We'll return to the Isaiah passage, so for now let's move ahead to Jesus' commission to the disciples. Note exactly whom Jesus commands to make disciples of all nations: the eleven disciples. We automatically apply this verse to all Christians and to the church in general, equating as we do the calling of the original disciples with our calling. But in a larger reading of the New Testament, this command is actually only given to the eleven disciples. This is the point at which the disciples—learners of Jesus—become apostles, those "sent out" to tell others about Jesus. These eleven very much become the first apostles.

But not every Christian is called to be an apostle. As Paul says in Ephesians when listing the gifts of the Holy Spirit, "The gifts he gave were that some would be apostles, some prophets, some evangelists, some pastors and teachers" (4:11, NRSV). *Some* are apostles, not all. Nor does he suggest here or anywhere in Ephesians that being sent out to the world is the main purpose of the church.

He specifically says that he is so called: "Although I am the very least of all the saints, this grace was given to me to bring to the Gentiles the news of the boundless riches of Christ" (Ephesians 3:8, NRSV). But he does not even hint that his calling is every Christian's calling or that of the church in general. It's his call and that of the other apostles.

So yes, there are people in the church called apostles who very much are called to go out into the world and preach and teach. And yes, there is a sense in which the teaching of God's people goes out into the world. And yes, there is a sense in which we are light and even salt for the world, as the passage from Isaiah so beautifully expresses. Let us not denigrate our evangelistic call.

But let me suggest that all this does not constitute *our very purpose* as the people of God. It is clearly the calling of some of the people of God, and so it must be the calling of others in the family of God to support them in their apostolic and evangelistic work through prayer and giving. But that is a far cry from this being the very purpose of the church, *the reason for its existence.*

You might wonder, What about Matthew 25, where Jesus speaks about the call to social justice? Jesus seems to suggest that the judgment of God at the end of history will be determined by our social justice efforts. What could indicate our purpose more than this?

Jesus describes a scene where people from all over the world are gathered before him at the judgment. He separates them into two groups, the sheep and the goats, and he says to the sheep,

> "Come, you that are blessed by my Father, inherit
> the kingdom prepared for you from the foundation
> of the world [notice the language here, the same as
> in Ephesians: before the foundation of the world
> God was preparing the Kingdom for himself], for I
> was hungry and you gave me food, I was thirsty and
> you gave me something to drink, I was a stranger
> and you welcomed me, I was naked and you gave me

clothing, I was sick and you took care of me, I was in prison and you visited me."

Then the righteous will answer him, "Lord, when was it that we saw you hungry and gave you food, or thirsty and gave you something to drink? And when was it that we saw you a stranger and welcomed you, or naked and gave you clothing? And when was it that we saw you sick or in prison and visited you?"

And the king will answer them, "Truly I tell you, just as you did it to one of the least of these who are members of my family, you did it to me."

MATTHEW 25:34-40, NRSV

This version has appropriately rendered the literal "brothers" as "members of my family." The people who need ministering to are not just people in general, anyone who suffers. The specific people in question are the people of God, the brothers and sisters of Christ, members of the family of God. The call to justice, in this instance, is not even a call to justice—no wrongs are being righted. It's a simple call for compassion for the people of God when they are in dire straits. It's a call for the church to be especially attentive to those in the family who suffer. It hearkens to Paul's injunction that we should "work for the good of all," but "especially for those of the family of faith" (Galatians 6:10, NRSV).

What about the prophetic passages from Isaiah, Jeremiah, Amos, and Micah? Don't they enjoin us to be concerned about social justice for all? What about all those harsh judgments against those who oppress widows and orphans and mistreat the sojourner, who accept bribes instead of doing justice? Is this not a clear and clarion call to work for justice in society?

Yes and no. One can hardly deny the need for Christians to work for justice in society. Any Christian whose heart does not break over injustice, who does nothing to alleviate suffering in the world, is likely not a Christian in the first place. But we'll come back to this.

In the case of the prophetic literature, we often fail to recognize that the prophets are little concerned about the treatment of widows and orphans and about bribes in Assyria, Babylon, and elsewhere. But they are very concerned about them in Israel and Judah, very concerned about these things as they are practiced *among the people of God*.

And why not, if the people of God are called to be a light to the nations? What type of light can they be if they act like everyone else? The call of the prophets is not that everyone, everywhere will pursue justice for all, but that the people of God would treat one another justly—righteously—in the presence of God.

Certainly the other nations come into view now and then in prophetic denouncements, but the overwhelming concern of the prophets is for the quality of life among God's chosen people.

Again, we need to make a distinction between one task the people of God are called to perform and the very ground of their being, the very purpose of their life together. We are by all means to love our neighbors, which now includes our enemies. One way we love them is through acts of mercy and justice. But this does not mean that the church exists for the sake of the world.

PAUL'S PROPHETIC SIDE

I find it interesting to see how Paul adapts the prophetic concern for righteousness among the people of God to the local situation in Ephesus. In this epistle, he is clearly concerned first and foremost about the quality of life of the people of God.

For example, what in Paul's mind are we supposed to do once we have been incorporated into the family of God? Note one summary that comes at the end of the classic passage on grace: "For by grace you have been saved through faith, and this is not your own doing; it is the gift of God—not the result of works, so that no one may boast. For we are what he has made us, created in Christ Jesus for good works, which God prepared beforehand to be our way of life" (Ephesians 2:8-10, NRSV).

From "beforehand"—which reverberates with chapter 1's "before the foundation of the world"—God prepared us, called us, saved us to do "good works." Earlier we saw that those predestined works were summarized like this: "he chose us in Christ before the foundation of the world to be holy and blameless before him in love" and "to live for the praise of his glory." Not holy and blameless in some abstract way, nor holy and blameless in morality in general. But to be holy and blameless in one specific thing: before God in love.

It should not surprise us, then, that just after Paul says

that we have been predestined for good works, he goes on to describe those good works primarily in terms of love:

> So then, remember that at one time you Gentiles by birth . . . were at that time without Christ, being aliens from the commonwealth of Israel, and strangers to the covenants of promise, having no hope and without God in the world. But now in Christ Jesus you who once were far off have been brought near by the blood of Christ. For he is our peace; in his flesh he has made both groups into one and has broken down the dividing wall, that is, the hostility between us. He has abolished the law with its commandments and ordinances, that he might create in himself one new humanity in place of the two, thus making peace, and might reconcile both groups to God in one body through the cross, thus putting to death that hostility through it.
>
> EPHESIANS 2:11-16, NRSV

Right after the line about good works, Paul begins talking about the new and amazing fact on the ground, that the people of God includes both Jews and Gentiles. Though formerly hostile to one another, that dividing wall between them has been demolished in Christ. Paul is anxious for his readers to see this utterly new situation: "I pray that you may have the power to comprehend, with all the saints, what is the breadth and length and height and depth, and to know the love of Christ that surpasses knowledge, so that you may be filled with all the fullness of God" (Ephesians 3:18-19, NRSV).

And in light of this new reality, he exhorts his readers, "I therefore, the prisoner in the Lord, beg you to lead a life worthy of the calling to which you have been called, with all humility and gentleness, with patience, bearing with one another in love, making every effort to maintain the unity of the Spirit in the bond of peace" (Ephesians 4:1-3, NRSV).

To summarize his argument: we all have been saved by grace. Through grace we are now called to live a life of good works, to be holy and blameless in love in the presence of God. Specifically that means we are to learn how to live in love and unity in the body of Christ, both Jews and Gentiles together, as we glorify God. We are to live with one another in humility and gentleness, with patience, to bear with one another in love, and to make every effort to maintain this unity in peace. These are the specific "good works" we are called to perform.

Since the church's identity—its very reason for being—is as a people who bask in the pleasure of being united to God in Christ and to one another, so that Christ "fills all in all" (Ephesians 1:23, NRSV), then right now, before that promise is fulfilled, we are called to live into that destiny. That means first and foremost learning to live in unity and love with one another as we praise his glory together in worship. This, it seems, is the equivalent of the prophetic call for the people of Israel to live righteously together.

We should note how this is the call of Jesus to all who believe in him. Note his prayer at the end of his earthly life.

It is the climax of his prayer, the destination of his prayer, what is most important for him to say at the end. He's not merely praying for his disciples (soon-to-be apostles) but for everyone who will come to believe in him:

> I ask not only on behalf of these, but also on behalf of those who will believe in me through their word, that they may all be one. As you, Father, are in me and I am in you, may they also be in us, so that the world may believe that you have sent me. The glory that you have given me I have given them, so that they may be one, as we are one, I in them and you in me, that they may become completely one, so that the world may know that you have sent me and have loved them even as you have loved me.
>
> JOHN 17:20-23, NRSV

The church's main horizontal "mission" (if we want to call it that) before Jesus' second coming is to live together in peace, to love one another, to do good works for one another, to be holy and blameless in love before God and one another, bridging the classic divides between Greeks and Jews, male and female, slave and free—and all in the context of worship, living for the praise of God's glory.

When we do this well, we are ever so faintly showing the life of the new Jerusalem, thus being a light to the nations, a sign of where history is headed, when God "will live with them, and they will be his people. God himself will be with them" (Revelation 21:3). Where Christ will fill all in all, so that all the family will bask in the sheer delight of his love, praising and glorifying him forever.

My conclusion after surveying the biblical landscape is this: the church's mission is not to go out and make the world a better place, to be a blessing, to transform culture, to bring justice to the earth, to work for human flourishing. The church's destiny and purpose is to live together in love in Christ, to the praise of God's glory. That, in fact, is the destiny of all humankind, no matter what corner of the globe they come from.

Rather than the world being the purpose for the church, the purpose of the world is to become the church.

CHAPTER 5

RETHINKING THE CHURCH: A MORE BALANCED DIET

THIS VIEW—that the church's mission is not first and foremost to go out and make the world a better place but to live together in love in Christ, to the praise of God's glory—is not just a theological construct, a creative way to think about the relationship of the church to the world. Based on my experience as a pastor and member of the mainline and on my three decades as a journalist embedded in American evangelicalism, I think this view of the church is crucial for the health and survival of American Christianity.

Here is what I've seen happen time and again when the church is conceived of as primarily missional, existing for the sake of the world.

First, it energizes many Christians—let's acknowledge

that. This was one motive of Rauschenbusch as he articulated the social gospel. And Newbigin's missional word to self-satisfied British churches woke many people up. I understand the attraction.

I've been in moribund, dying churches that are transformed when they adopt a missional stance—at least for a time. When a church congregation comes to believe that the church is to make a difference in the world, the members make a shift that is exciting. It lights a fire under them, giving them new meaning and purpose. They enthusiastically give themselves ever more deeply to the church, because they now think the church is going to make a difference in the world. Naturally, they imagine, the church is going to shape itself and its organization to transform the world.

What they eventually discover, however, is that churches rarely do this. The church fails to give more to missions. It fails to reorganize itself missionally. It keeps investing in worship and Christian education and discipleship at the expense of reaching out to the surrounding culture. This disappointment is felt in many quarters and felt especially keenly by those who assume a missional call for the church. Book after book and missional conference after missional conference are dedicated to addressing this problem.

A handful of churches do, in fact, turn themselves into missional organizations but usually only for a short period. The missional minded become discouraged and angry at this point. They accuse the church of hypocrisy, selfishness, and irrelevance. While such is true of the church in all times and places—we are sinners, after all—what many fail to recognize is this reality: the church is actually not designed to be missional.

To be clear, let me say what I mean by "the church." I understand church to be a concrete body of believers gathered to worship God in Christ, gathered around the preached and taught Word and sacraments/ordinances like the Lord's Supper and baptism, living together and growing in love. Most of us instinctively understand this as "church," even though we might acknowledge that parachurch organizations, with their specialized ministries, are composed of members of the family of God and therefore, by extension, can be called "the church." But here, I focus on the concrete reality of the local, worshiping congregation as the preeminent expression of the church.

Let me give an example that suggests why the church is not designed to be missional at its core. It's something I've seen happen in many churches. A church hires a youth minister, and the church and youth minister write up a missional job description: the youth minister's main job is to reach out to troubled youth in the community and bring them to Christ. Many church members applaud this missional approach, and they pat him on the back and tell him to get started.

So he goes out to the local high schools and hangs out with various lost souls, inviting them into the church. But the youth minister finds that it takes an extraordinary amount of time and energy to minister to this group. The better he reaches out missionally to lost teens, the less time he has to disciple the youth of the congregation. Naturally, parents of the church's youth are anxious for their teenagers to grow in Christ, and they thought that in part they had hired the youth minister to help do that. But this youth minister is usually nowhere to be found, because he's out in the community ministering to unchurched youth.

You see where this is going. It is clear that (a) troubled youth need Christians to reach out to them, (b) Christian youth need teaching and nurturing, and (c) it is the rare situation in which a youth minister can do both effectively. The church is simply not set up to do both, and if my biblical argument in the previous chapter is correct, it is not *supposed* to do both in the same sort of way. The primary purpose of a youth minister in my reading is to help youth become holy and blameless in love, doing so in the context of praising God's glory in worship.

This makes some of us squirm because it feels so selfish, as if the church is deserting the world. But it turns out that the church is not a very efficient institution for making a difference in the world. If you are passionate about feeding the hungry, for example, churches can help here and there. But if you really want to make a difference—really cut the numbers of the hungry and malnourished—it's more effective to give your time to a government or business or nonprofit agency that specializes in such things.

For example, global poverty rates plunged from 43 percent of the world population in 1990 to 22 percent in 2008 to 10 percent in 2015. How do experts account for this dramatic turn? Churches and nonprofits may have played a role, but overwhelmingly it was governments (especially in China and India) making "pro-poor investments"—that is, creating market conditions for growth, investing in technology, and increasing education.[1] Such initiatives require billions of dollars and economic and technological expertise far beyond the abilities of any church or group of churches. If you really want to defeat poverty, you're better off starting a business or getting elected to an office that can change laws.

The same is true whether we're talking about sex trafficking, drug abuse, exploitation of labor, environmental degradation, or any of a number of other social issues. The church as church can make a donation, organize a committee, or sponsor a food closet, but it cannot really make a significant, lasting impact. It is not set up to do that. In fact, it has many other important jobs to do.

More than anything, it is called, for example, to provide a time and place for the public worship of God and for people to receive the sacraments/ordinances of baptism and the Lord's Supper—to meet God as we glorify him. It is also called to teach children, youth, and adults about who God is as well as the shape and nature of the Christian life. It is a place where Christians gather to receive mutual encouragement and prayer. It's the place where we learn to live into our destiny: to be holy and blameless in love to the praise of God's glory.

This does not mean the church is free to ignore, for example, troubled and unchurched youth. Far from it. But the church is not the institution best suited to reach out to them. This is one reason I've been a big fan, big contributor, and board member of my local Young Life ministry—they do a great job at that. Parachurch organizations are great at specialized outreach.

But what about those people whose hopes for a missional church have been dashed? What happens to them, and what happens to the church?

In my experience, what happens is that many give up on the church. Because their vision of the church is missional, the church, in their view, has simply failed, and so they stop coming. Instead, they give more and more of their time to specialty institutions (parachurch ministries and other nonprofits) or throw themselves into politics—which is about nothing else but making the world a better place. If it has been ingrained in you that the church was created for the world, that your purpose is to make the world a better place, why bother with the church? It is clearly not very effective. Better to give yourself to UNICEF or the Democratic party.

And this is precisely what so many in the mainline have done over the last several decades. There are many reasons for the numerical decline of mainline Christianity, but in my mind, one of the main ones is that somewhere in the 1960s mainliners grabbed afresh the idea that the church was created for the sake of the world, that the purpose of the church was to make the world a better place. It led to initial enthusiasm, yes, but then despair as it became apparent that, other than making political pronouncements at annual conventions, the church was ill-equipped to make the world a better place. When the children of that generation put two and two together, they saw they could chuck the church and still go about trying to make a difference without it.

But something else happens when churches recognize how bad they are at being missional. Many of them double down. They see young people leaving the church in droves because it isn't relevant to the world, because it isn't making a difference in the world, and these churches panic. Unfortunately, they continue to assume that to be relevant means to make this a better world. And so they shout it even more from the rooftops, and they make more pronouncements about more and more social ills, the more recent the better. The tone of their theology becomes ever more secular. Then you find more and more that the mainline churches look like nothing more than the Democratic party at prayer, and evangelical churches like the Republican party at worship.

Today it seems clear to me that many of the evangelical left are traveling down the path hewn by the mainline. And the evangelical right—starting with Jerry Falwell and the rise of the religious right—have been on the path hewn by civil religion, a religion of God and country. Both left and right are anxious to make a difference in the world, to make the world a better place according to their own lights, because they both believe that the purpose of the church is to make the world a better place. Instead, in my view, they will end up marginalizing the church even more.

What I predict for evangelicalism in particular is what I've seen happen to the mainline. The more we are fascinated with the missional, and the more we take this medicine as the fix for the malady of church sluggishness, the more sick we are going to become, and the more people in our midst will become frustrated. And that will lead to still more people leaving the church.

We can already see signs of it. More than ten years ago, Michael Lindsay researched and wrote a now classic survey of evangelical cultural influencers: *Faith in the Halls of Power: How Evangelicals Joined the American Elite.*[2] In the course of his research, he discovered that a large number of evangelicals were embedded in key cultural institutions— government, education, entertainment, and so forth—and that they were, in fact, making a difference in the world. But he also noticed how few of them were connected to a local church.

Let me hazard a guess that these cultural leaders found the local church irrelevant, likely to their own spiritual growth but also because it was not making a difference in the world. Since that book, the number of those who identify as "spiritual but not religious" has only increased, which suggests that the Christians in this group are even less committed to the church, and I suspect for the same reasons.

There is no question that some churches are on life support, and some have become spiritual social clubs. Some churches have hurt and even abused members physically, psychologically, or spiritually. Those are understandable reasons to leave a church and not come back for years. But I suspect a high percentage of people who leave evangelical churches do so because they do not think the church is doing enough to make a difference in the world.

WHERE SAINTS ARE MADE

These evangelical elite have paved the way for all those believers who live a churchless Christianity and serve God through other institutions. What these Christians do in the world is right and good and truly to be admired. They are indeed loving their neighbors in inspirational ways.

What concerns me is that so many have deserted the one institution that embodies the very purpose of God for the world. And what saddens me is that they have removed themselves from the one place that can teach them about love as can no other.

In Paul's vision, the church is composed of people of all stripes and sins and persuasions and ethnicities and races and strengths and weaknesses but united in Christ. Given this, I can think of no institution on the planet that is better situated to teach its members to live in love.

One is tempted at this point to paint an idealistic picture of the church. But that is precisely what we must not do. We don't have to wait for the church to live into its ideals to see that it already is the testing ground for the biblical vision. I only have to ask you to think about your own church, and you'll get the point.

Your church probably has a Max, a legalist who reads the Bible literally and endlessly criticizes everything that isn't proven from the Bible. Then there's Marjorie, a woman who works mightily in Sunday school but whose weakness is gossip, some of which you've been the subject of. Then there's that couple, David and Barbara, separated while they try to work things out. On the mission committee Doris and Jim repeatedly argue, sometimes not charitably, about whether to give more money to evangelistic or social justice causes. You also suspect the associate pastor may have a drinking problem. And you've never gotten along with Scott because he's so fanatical about the environment.

And on it goes. And yet every Sunday, you gather together with this motley crew to worship Jesus Christ. You pray together; you sing hymns that speak of your unity in Christ; you affirm your common faith in God—Father, Son, and Holy Spirit; you pass the peace or welcome one another as a sign of your love. You sit on committees, attend Bible studies, and serve food at the homeless shelter with these people. You live with them in something resembling a community centered on Jesus. It's not pretty. It's not glorious. But it is a laboratory of love, where God is met and relationships are endured, worked at, and rejoiced in. It's a place where saints are made.

It's also the main place that regularly reminds us to love our neighbors. Let's not forget that. The fact that loving neighbors is not the church's primary mission does not mean it is not still the second great commandment for disciples. So the church encourages its members to practice simple acts of hospitality as well as acts of sacrifice for those outside the church. It encourages us to volunteer with Habitat for Humanity and to staff the local food pantry or homeless shelter. Perhaps some church members will run for Congress or join the police force or teach in the inner city. Some will become doctors or lawyers, others grocers and gardeners—all of whom for the rest of the week work in the Spirit of the Lord in their various vocations to make the world a better place.

If you want to do something that is really hard, and if you want to push yourself to the limits, if you want to be constantly tested to love, if you want to live into your ultimate destiny—if you want to learn to be holy and blameless in love before God—there is no better place to do that than in the local church.

Many of us today rightly note the great defects in the church, most of which boil down to its superficiality. Because the church thinks it has to be missional, that it has to be a place where the world feels comfortable, it has dumbed down the preaching and the worship so that in many quarters we have ended up with a lowest-common-denominator Christianity. It goes down easy, which is why it attracts so many and why many churches are growing. But it is a meal designed to stunt the growth of the people of God. And it is a way of church life that eventually burns people out, where people become exhausted trying to make the world a better place.

What if instead the church was a sanctuary, a place of rest, where the fellowship of believers lived together in love? What if we let parachurch organizations and other vocations be where we serve the unchurched neighbor and, by God's grace, make a difference in their world, and the church be the place where we learn to be holy and blameless in love before God?

It's not that learning to love in the church is all that easy.

But learning to love has this self-generating quality: the more we fail, the more we turn to God and others for forgiveness and thus imbibe the life-changing power of grace.

If this biblical vision settles into more and more local churches—and it's already present in many places—I believe we would see some significant changes. The church would no longer be a place that is anxious and worried about being relevant to the world on the world's terms; it wouldn't worry about its inability to make a difference by society's norms; it wouldn't think of itself as a means to a useful end but as God's end for humanity—that is, a place where we learn to live together in love: Republican and Democrat, rich and poor, male and female, white and Hispanic and black and Asian. A place where we would learn to grow up into the stature and fullness of Christ, who is all in all, to the praise of God's glory.

And more than anything, it would become a place where we learn everything there is to know about praising God's glory, a place where we learn the fine art of praise, a place that would employ every form of music and word and drama and reading and visual art to praise God for his coming salvation, so that when the nations of the world flood into the new Jerusalem, they will have songs to sing and chants to chant and words to praise the God who has brought them together in love.

This, I believe, is the purpose of the church. And in the next several chapters, we will look more closely at how this vision could affect the various facets of church life.

CHAPTER 6

THE FOCUS
OF WORSHIP

THE ABSOLUTE BEST WORSHIP SERVICE I have ever been to was in an Orthodox church in downtown Chicago. It was full of evangelical converts to Orthodoxy, so it had the rich, historic liturgy and singing combined with evangelical fervor. I daresay I felt lifted into the presence of God, or better, that the presence of God had descended on us.

The absolute worst worship service I have ever attended was in an Orthodox church in Philadelphia. The priests led the liturgy from behind the iconostasis—a screen of icons separating the sanctuary (where the altar sits) from the nave (where the congregation sits). The only response the congregation was called to make was the occasional amen. We didn't even join the priests in singing. My Protestant sensibilities were so offended, I walked out in the middle of the service.

I relate this experience to say that even though I believe that Orthodoxy in general exalts and glorifies God like no other Christian tradition, even a tradition that has all the right "tools" for adoration can stumble.

And this brings us to evangelical worship, which has its own highs and lows. Our understandable and often impressive yearning is to take the love of God into the world. Yet Scripture is clear that our first call is to stand in the presence of our loving God and worship him. Again, as the Westminster Shorter Catechism puts it, our chief end is "to glorify God and to enjoy him forever."

The framers of that well-known line were deeply influenced by the sweep of biblical history and the end toward which history moves.

First note that, depending on how one numbers them, three or four of the Ten Commandments are about proper worship:

> You must not have any other god but me.
> You must not make for yourself an idol of
>   any kind. . . .
> You must not misuse the name of the LORD
>   your God. . . .
> Remember to observe the Sabbath.
>
> EXODUS 20:3-4, 7-8

If that were not enough, add to that the many detailed laws prescribing how the Temple was to be built and adorned and how worship was to be conducted. God apparently did not think that any detail was too small when it came to worship. Take, for example, the instructions regarding the table that was to hold the Bread of the Presence:

> Make a table of acacia wood, 36 inches long,
> 18 inches wide, and 27 inches high. Overlay it with
> pure gold and run a gold molding around the edge.
> Decorate it with a 3-inch border all around, and
> run a gold molding along the border. Make four
> gold rings for the table and attach them at the four
> corners next to the four legs. Attach the rings near
> the border to hold the poles that are used to carry
> the table.
>
> EXODUS 25:23-28

Then there is the book of Psalms, which was and continues to be used as a hymnbook for worship.

To be sure, in the Prophets, the Lord chastises his people for their fastidious worship, especially when their so-called devotion to God was not matched by the love of neighbor. And so we find God often saying, in one way or another, that true worship is to seek justice for the oppressed. Ethics, however, never replaces adoration in the Prophets but is seen as a necessary complement to true worship. In the end, it's all about worship. As the prophet Micah records,

> In the last days, the mountain of the LORD's house
> will be the highest of all—
> the most important place on earth.

It will be raised above the other hills,
    and people from all over the world will stream
       there to worship.

MICAH 4:1

This vision of the end of history—meaning both its destination and its purpose—is hardly abandoned in the New Testament. From Paul's vision of every knee bowing and every tongue confessing Jesus as Lord (see Philippians 2:10-11) to John's vision of the twenty-four elders glorifying God (see Revelation 4) and many places between, we see worship as the great and wondrous activity in the Kingdom of Heaven.

In the last decade or so, evangelical congregations have woken up to the centrality of praise and adoration. One of the great developments of our time is how we worship. "Praise choruses" and contemporary worship music, for all their limitations, aim our hearts and minds in the direction of God. We do not even have to be taught to lift our faces or raise our arms as we sing these songs, as the songs themselves often drive us upward to seek and praise God. You would have to be a spiritual miser not to recognize how such music has helped the church worship God.

Yet the temptation of the horizontal is with us always, and it comes in many disguises in our worship. Unfortunately, worship leaders—as they themselves often admit—are tempted to take cues from Finney's *Lectures on Revivals*. Every worship leader worth his or her salt knows how to manage the emotions of the congregation, moving them from quiet devotion to raucous praise, or from bass-throbbing adulation to whisper-quiet meditation. We don't have to deny that, despite sometimes obvious manipulation, we've been touched by God in such services. But it is a constant temptation to replace God with technique, to seek not the Holy of Holies but to enjoy spiritual jollies.

Another way of putting this temptation is this: what we often really want is for worship to give us a good spiritual feeling. I suspect this because of our inattention to what we're singing.

We sing various choruses that say, "Bring down your glory" and "Show us your face." But we do not know what we're asking for. People in the Bible who actually encounter God's glory fall on the ground in fear. For example, after the miraculous catch of fish, Peter knows he is in the presence of the Glorious One. He doesn't give God an ovation. He doesn't weep with joy. He falls on his knees, begging Jesus to depart from him. The glory of Jesus has made it clear to him that he is a sinful man (see Luke 5:1-11).

The same thing happens to Isaiah in the Temple. When Isaiah is given but a glimpse of God's glory, he doesn't break into a praise chorus. He actually thinks he is about to die: "It's all over! I am doomed, for I am a sinful man. I have filthy lips, and I live among a people with filthy lips. Yet I have seen the King, the LORD of Heaven's Armies" (Isaiah 6:5).

In fact, God refuses to allow Moses to see his face precisely because it will lead to Moses' demise (see Exodus 33:20).

Even more sobering is the connection that John's Gospel makes with divine glory. John's Gospel is certainly in part about the display of Jesus' miraculous powers—but they weren't so spectacular as to prevent some from unbelief, Jesus' glory is a quiet, humble glory that is impossible to discern without faith. And this also is glory: the humility of the Incarnation and the degradation of the Crucifixion.

When we ask for God's glory, we are not asking to know the fear of God and the humble suffering that life in him entails. If we're honest with ourselves, we mostly want a good religious feeling. We really aren't interested in what God's glory is and what it might do to us.

But let me be fair. What we're often asking for in such praise songs is to know God intimately, personally, and immediately. In this regard, we are very much in tune with the psalmist, who pants after God. We are wise to note, however, that if we get what we ask for, it's going to be more complex and paradoxical than we can imagine. That's why it's another good sign that more and more churches are trying to integrate classic hymns into their offerings, as these do more often speak to God's fullness and complexity.

How we actually shape our services points to another horizontal temptation. Many churches, for example, have more or less structured worship around two cultural icons: the rock concert and late-night comedy. On the one hand, many evangelical churches have a typical band—guitars, bass, electric piano, and drums, along with singers—performing up front. "No, they are leading worship, not performing," some might object. But let's face it, there is a performative element in everything that happens on the stage. Yes, the band intends to lead us in worship, but we've all been to services where the music is so loud that we cannot hear the person next to us singing. As much as worship leaders strive to keep their egos in check, they are the first to admit that the very ambiance of contemporary worship makes it nearly impossible for people to not think of them as rock stars—of worship, yes, but rock stars nonetheless.

Even churches committed to more classical, liturgical worship find the temptation to imitate a rock concert irresistible. One Anglican church I'm familiar with, when remodeling a building to worship in, planted the drum set not off to the side with the other musicians but right in front of the large cross that adorns the center of the stage. In a tradition that grasps the importance of symbols and how they can help us worship, adore God, and draw us into his presence, the imagery is shocking. As worship continues, where will people's eyes focus: on the cross that stands still or on the drummer who is moving rhythmically with the music? The clashing symbolism is distracting, to say the least.

This, by the way, is one of the most effective churches in the community for reaching out to the lost and hurting in the name of Christ. Yet this illustrates how confused we are about the relationship between the horizontal and the vertical—and the confusing messages we end up sending to ourselves and to those who visit our churches.

And it isn't as if traditional, liturgical churches have any advantage here. Having been a long-standing member of Episcopal and Anglican churches, I can assure you that it's not unusual for postworship conversation to concern itself with whether some liturgical action or word was done properly, followed by a word to the priest that such-and-such acolyte needs more training. Or take one extreme example—how to light the small fire kindled at the church's entrance as a prelude to the Easter vigil. I remember one otherwise loving and compassionate deacon who was in deep distress with an interim priest who lit the Easter fire with a pocket lighter—as if doing so was sacrilege. So yes, a focus on the horizontal can tempt the liturgical as well.

Despite the renewed focus on adoration as a key element in evangelical worship, I suspect that we're still more interested in the horizontal than the vertical many days. How many times have we heard someone say the traditional picture of heaven sounds pretty boring, like one long worship service? That says something about what we think of our worship services and what we think of worship. As Puritan theologian Isaac Ambrose put it, "Consider that *looking unto Jesus* is the work of heaven. . . . If then we like not this work, how will we live in heaven?"[1] Instead, when we want to make the Kingdom of Heaven sound more attractive, we talk about it like this: "Whatever you enjoy doing in this life—athletics, woodworking, art, gardening, baking, etc.—will be extraordinary in the life to come." Or we look forward to a glad reunion with loved ones.

Those sorts of things do seem to be part of the glorious age to come. What signals a problem is our hearts. Who of us will not admit that it's these activities and the reunion with loved ones that often get us more excited than spending eternity glorifying the True, the Good, and the Beautiful One?

Rethinking how we do worship begins, then, with keeping the focus on God from beginning to end. Experienced worship leaders will have the best ideas about how to do this, so I won't add to their wisdom.

I do think one key is to recognize that everything that happens in the service is worship, and not just the music. Many of us have gotten into the terrible theological habit of calling only the first part of our services "worship," when we are singing praise to God in three or four songs. We say things like, "Before we listen to the sermon, let's spend some time in worship." As if the singing is about God and the sermon is not. This is a confusion of the first order. The sermon is also supposed to be about God first and foremost. That's why traditionally the entire service—singing, prayer, Bible reading, preaching, offering, and benediction—is referred to as *worship*.

So that's one perception we might change. Another has to do with the sacraments/ordinances, which deserves its own chapter.

CHAPTER 7

WHAT EVER HAPPENED TO COMMUNION?

THERE IS NO GREATER SIGNAL that evangelicals have long forgotten their roots than the disrepair into which the sacraments (or ordinances) have fallen in our day. By way of reminder, we should note that the Second Great Awakening began as a Communion retreat. Churches from all over gathered at Cane Ridge, Kentucky, to prepare themselves for and then partake in Communion. I wrote an article about this revival many years ago:

> Communions (annual three-to-five-day meetings climaxed with the Lord's Supper) gathered people in the dozens, maybe the hundreds. At this Cane Ridge Communion, though, sometimes 20,000 people

swirled about the grounds—watching, praying, preaching, weeping, groaning, falling. Though some stood at the edges and mocked, most left marveling at the wondrous hand of God.

The Cane Ridge Communion quickly became one of the best-reported events in American history, and according to Vanderbilt historian Paul Conkin, "arguably . . . the most important religious gathering in all of American history." It ignited the explosion of evangelical religion, which soon reached into nearly every corner of American life. For decades the prayer of camp meetings and revivals across the land was "Lord, make it like Cane Ridge."

At such Communions, people gathered on Friday and spent that evening and Saturday praying, reading Scripture, and listening to sermons as they prepared themselves for worship and Communion on Sunday. At Cane Ridge, Saturday was not so quiet:

> The Saturday morning services had been quiet—the proverbial lull before a storm. But by afternoon, the preaching was continual, from both the meetinghouse and the tent. . . . Excitement mounted, and amid smoke and sweat, the camp erupted in noise: the cries and shouts of the penitent, the crying of babies, the shrieking of children, and the neighing of horses.

Then the tumultuous bodily "exercises" began.
Along with the shouting and crying, some began
falling. Some experienced only weakened knees or
a light head (including Governor James Garrard).
Others fell but remained conscious or talkative;
a few fell into a deep coma, displaying the symptoms
of a grand mal seizure or a type of hysteria. Though
only a minority fell, some parts of the grounds were
strewn like a battlefield.

Some were attended to where they fell; others
were carried to a convenient place, where people
would gather around them to pray and sing
hymns. "If they [the fallen] speak," one reported,
"what they say is attended to, being very solemn
and affecting—many are struck under such
exhortations. . . ."

Early Sunday morning, relative calm reigned,
though some had been up most of the night. The
central purpose of the gathering—the Communion—
took place as scheduled in the meetinghouse. The
minister of a nearby congregation preached the
traditional sermon outside, and then those with
Communion tokens went inside for the sacrament.
The tables, set up in the shape of a cross in the aisles,
could probably accommodate 100 at a time. Over
the ensuing hours, hundreds were served. [Minister
John] Lyle wrote that he had "clearer views of divine
things than . . . before" as he partook, and that he
felt "uncommonly tender" as he spoke.[1]

The point of rehearsing this history is not to suggest that we should try to create emotionally extravagant Communion services like this. Clearly, that was a unique moment in American church history. But what impresses me is the reverence and seriousness with which these believers approached Communion, a reverence and seriousness seldom seen today.

THE LOW STATE OF THE SACRAMENTS

Let me begin by clarifying my use of the term *sacrament*. Some evangelical churches call the Lord's Supper and baptism *ordinances*, to suggest they are actions Jesus commands us to participate in and that they signal our faith in and obedience to Christ. The term *sacrament* includes these two ideas and another crucial one: that they are means of grace. By "means of grace," I'm not proposing any specific theology—whether transubstantiation or consubstantiation, whether real or symbolic presence. But for all believers, Communion and baptism are practices in which one's faith is deepened and strengthened, and that sort of thing only happens by God's grace. This is what I mean by "means of grace" in this chapter, and it is why I will use the word *sacrament* to talk about them.

As I said, I believe these sacraments are in a profoundly low state in many areas of evangelical church life.

Take baptism. Even among churches that believe Matthew 28:19 is the church's rallying cry ("Go and make disciples of all the nations, *baptizing* them"), the sacrament is no longer central to their mission. It would be difficult to come by statistics that suggest the problem, but one anecdote suggests it's a serious one. I belong to an Anglican church in Wheaton, Illinois, which meets not far from Wheaton College. The charismatic singing and Bible-centered preaching attract many Wheaton College students to attend worship and to become members. However, to partake in Communion, as well as to become a member, a person must have been baptized. The pastors are continually amazed at the number of Wheaton College students—no doubt some of the most earnest, devout, and intelligent young people of the evangelical world—who have yet to be baptized. One would have thought that their churches had attended to this matter long before they left home for college.

Another sign of the problem is the deep fear some evangelicals have that baptism might be anything more than a symbol or a declaration. I attended an independent church in Dallas, Texas, on a Sunday when they were having a mass baptism for some four hundred people. This speaks well of the effectiveness of their outreach and their desire to obey the commands of their Lord. As part of the service, four or five people came on stage and were interviewed by the pastor to help them give their testimony. And at the end of each testimony, the last question the pastor asked was, "But you don't believe that baptism saves you, right?" The leading way in which he asked this question suggested to me that the pastor was deeply afraid that the sacrament might be anything more than merely symbolic. And the fact that he also asked this right before each person was baptized went a long way toward ensuring that the sacrament remained all about the horizontal—a display of the person's faith to others—rather than allowing for the possibility that God might break in and bless the recipient.

The Lord's Supper is in an even worse state. I've lost track of the number of start-up evangelical churches—again, who are sincerely seeking to reach the world for Christ—whose practice of Communion is frankly a sacrilege. One has to give them credit for, yes, seeking out the lost and taking down unnecessary cultural and religious barriers. And one has to also praise them for at least offering Communion. But in many churches, it is something that is presented during the offering at a small table holding crackers and juice in the side aisles for those who feel led to partake. Sometimes this is accompanied by the words of institution, but sometimes it is not.

The idea of *Communion*—of the body of Christ participating with one another in an ordinance of their Lord—is completely lost, not to mention the loss of any concerted effort by worship leaders to highlight why the sacrament is a central feature of Christian life.

In contrast to the evangelical churches of the late 1700s, it almost goes without saying that few if any evangelical congregations today would dedicate a whole weekend to preparing for and then participating in Communion. It would not only be perceived as a turnoff to unbelievers but a meaningless rite to members. And yet it was at Communions that thousands upon thousands came to know Christ intimately for the first time.

To be sure, there are evangelical churches today, high

church and low, Anglican and Baptist, who take the Lord's Supper with utmost seriousness. They—no matter their theology of the sacrament—will say it remains a means by which they are drawn out of themselves to remember the one who didn't just come to give them affirming spiritual feelings but died on a cross for their sins and rose again for their salvation.

We do well to recall the emphasis that our Baptist brothers and sisters insist on: that these are practices *ordained by our Lord*: "Go . . . baptizing in the name of the Father, Son, and Holy Spirit" and "Do this in remembrance of me." I do not believe evangelicalism will recover from its spiritual stupor, its fascination with the horizontal, until it once again practices regularly and respectfully, with earnestness and devotion, the sacraments of baptism and the Lord's Supper. Until, that is, it obeys the clear commands of its Lord.

As for the way forward—well, a lot depends on a particular church's theology of baptism and the Lord's Supper. But let me hazard some suggestions.

First, I don't think any sophisticated theology of Communion would make it an individualistic act as it has become in some churches. Simply refusing to offer Communion unless it is part of the service and everyone is invited—that's a start.

Against all odds, a church might very well offer a weekend retreat in which the focus is Communion—with teaching and times of prayer to prepare—and the climax being the receiving of the bread and cup.

As far as baptism is concerned, let's insist that as soon as possible, as infants or after conversion (whatever your theology), we obey the plain command of our Lord to baptize. And then when we do baptize, let's not get in the way of the act, by either overexplaining it or explaining it away. There is a time and place to teach a church's theology of baptism, but during the baptism we should let the visual power of the sacrament speak for itself. You can believe that baptism as such has no ultimate efficacy and still recognize that it is a powerful symbol.

In the context of this book, one reason I advocate the regular and reverential participation in the sacraments is because, as noted above, they require us to look at what is happening at the altar or Communion table or at the waters of baptism. We are required to look outside ourselves, to the physical means by which Christ blesses his people. Rather than encouraging us to ponder the feelings that are going on inside us or to look at others around us, the sacraments require us, however briefly, to focus on God and what he has done for us in Jesus Christ.

CHAPTER 8

BACK TO THE BIBLE

ONE SUNDAY when I lived in Fresno, California, I decided to visit two churches of contrasting styles. The first was the largest Presbyterian church in town. The second was the largest Assemblies of God church. Both were considered evangelical in doctrine and ethos. At the Presbyterian, I expected a quiet and reverential service, but instead was subjected to, among other light moments, a humorous skit on their upcoming vacation Bible school program that aroused great glee. At the Assemblies of God, I expected a lively service but found myself in reverential worship from start to finish.

What surprised me at both was how little Scripture was read. A Presbyterian service usually features Old Testament, Psalm, Epistle, and Gospel readings; this service included only a couple of verses from one of Paul's letters. The Assemblies service had a long reading from the New Testament but nothing from any other part of the Bible.

I had a similar experience in Dallas one Sunday. I visited a church whose pastor was famous for expository, biblical preaching, yet the Scripture reading for the day was a mere two verses.

And it's not uncommon in evangelical churches for the preacher to use the Bible merely as a jumping-off point to talk about whatever is considered urgent or relevant, like how to have a strong marriage or how to manage finances or what to do about racial injustice.

Such sermons drag in Bible verses that seem to speak to practical issues, but if you analyze the sermon, you quickly discern that the verses are mere ornamentation. That is, if you take out the verses, it really doesn't change the content of the sermon. What the preacher has done is simply talk about commonsense advice, advice that is available to anyone interested in the topic.

It's a good thing that churches give wise advice about practical matters and encourage us to work in the public square. Wisdom in daily life is something we all need, and it's not hard to see how this can be a hook to invite the unchurched to a service. And it's no surprise that such practical advice is supported by some Bible verses. But let's be honest: if the bulk of such sermons are about what we should and shouldn't do, the teaching is mostly about us, and the Bible turns into a book mostly about us and what we should do.

Given this phenomenon in evangelical churches, we

cannot remind ourselves too often that the Bible is first and foremost about God. How God created the world. How God called Abraham, redeemed the chosen people from slavery in Egypt, sent them into exile, and then rescued them again. How God came to us in Jesus Christ to die and rise again on our behalf. How God sent us the Holy Spirit and promises to bring history to a glorious conclusion. We believe the Bible is "the revelation of God," and by that we mean two things: it is revealed *by God*, and it is a revelation of *who God is*. The Bible is about God.

Unfortunately, that would not be clear to a first-time visitor to many evangelical churches, nor does it become apparent week by week. As I've said, we too often use the Bible as merely a starting point to talk about ourselves.

In small groups, the Bible is often used as a doorway to get us to talk about our inner lives. In this respect, I stand ashamed. In my early ministry, I can't count the number of times I took my cues for how to lead small-group Bible studies from books that majored in this technique. So we'd read about Jesus stilling the storm in Mark 4, and of course, the first question was "What are the storms in your life?" We'd talk about ourselves for an hour or so and then end with a brief prayer asking Jesus to calm our storms. But what made the evening interesting to all of us, the hook that kept us coming each week, was that we found ourselves in a fellowship of people who liked to talk about themselves and their struggles.

This dysfunction was embarrassingly revealed to me one evening as I led a small group of Laotian refugees in a Bible study on Mark 4. Our church had sponsored them as they made their way to America and sought refuge here, and they were interested in becoming members of the church. I was leading them through the Gospel of Mark to make sure they understood the Jesus they would be committing themselves to. After we read the passage aloud in English and Lao, I summarized the story and then asked my first question: "So what are the storms in your life?" The translator put the question in Lao, but everyone looked puzzled.

So I expanded. "What are the storms in your life, the areas that trouble you, cause you confusion, make you worried?" Again, blank stares. Then they started talking among themselves in emphatic tones.

I asked the translator what was going on. She said they were wondering if Jesus did indeed still a storm.

I said, "Well, yes." But I didn't want to get bogged down with the problem of miracles and the intellectual debate around it. I wanted to move the conversation into something personal and practical. So I said something like "But what we really should be thinking about is how Jesus can calm the storms in our lives."

There was a pause as they took this in, and then one of the men, through the translator, said with a measure of awe in his voice, "If Jesus stilled a storm, he must be a very powerful person."

I was stunned and not a little embarrassed. They had grasped the real meaning of this passage in the Gospel of Mark. Mark has, among other things, already shown that Jesus has authority to forgive sins (2:1-12), is Lord of the

Sabbath (2:23-28), and has authority over the demonic world (3:20-30). In Mark 4, the Gospel writer is showing that Jesus is Lord over all creation—even the wind and seas obey him.

Mark wants to tell us about Jesus. I wanted to talk about us, and I was shoehorning Mark to fit my agenda. Unfortunately, we pastors and teachers are tempted to do this all too often.

And we wonder why so many of our churches are characterized by moralistic therapeutic deism, a term coined by sociologist Christian Smith to summarize the latent beliefs of hundreds of evangelical youth he researched in the early 2000s. Despite their formal attachment to otherwise biblically orthodox churches, what youth really believed was that God was rarely if ever involved in day-to-day life—more like the deist God of many of America's founding fathers, who believed that God started the universe like a person winds a clock and then simply lets it run on its own. But more to the point here, the main purpose of faith for these youth was to teach people how to live rightly (moralistic) and to give them comfort and strength in life's challenges (therapeutic). Smith concluded that these youth were raised in churches in which most of the teaching and preaching focused on such matters.[1]

LOOKING FOR CHRIST IN
ALL SORTS OF PASSAGES

To counteract this dysfunction, many evangelical scholars and teachers have become enamored with the historical-critical reading of Scripture. I distinctly remember how my professors at Fuller scoffed at what they called "the spiritual reading" of a passage, in which readers immediately look for the spiritual lesson from a text before considering issues of literary context and purpose. A historical-critical reading (in all its various disciplines—form criticism, textual criticism, rhetorical criticism, etc.) helps to pull us out of ourselves and encourages us to read the Bible through the lens of the original biblical authors, to discern *their* intent rather than our own in reading Scripture.

This method, first developed in the nineteenth century among European and American liberals, has won the day among many evangelical pastors and teachers. And for good reason: it has indeed given us keen insights into the meaning of many passages of Scripture. We now see more clearly, for example, how each Gospel writer shaped his work to bring out some unique aspects of our Lord's life and ministry— how Matthew structures his Gospel to show Jesus as the ful- fillment of the Law and the Prophets, how Luke highlights the role of women and mercy, how John presents a cosmic Christ, and so on.

It has also helped us make more intelligent use of the Old Testament, to understand the larger religious and political contexts that help us see the uniqueness of God's revelation to Israel—how unique, for example, the radical monotheism of Israel was in a world saturated with polytheism.

Where this emphasis so often takes us, however, is strangely similar to the therapeutic reading that tempts us. The therapeutic reading focuses on us at the expense of God; a historical-critical reading can so emphasize the historical (the context of the original passage) and the critical (what various scholars say about the passage) that God becomes a bit player again. So we're tempted to spend an inordinate amount of time explaining the various sources of the Pentateuch, or labeling each psalm, or dividing up Isaiah into first and second if not third editions, or debating the historicity of Job or Jonah rather than engaging with what these texts say about God.

I once preached on a passage from Jonah to a congregation that had been nurtured on the historical-critical method by its previous pastor. But I completely ignored the historical-critical question in my sermon—neither defending Jonah's historicity nor denying it. Instead, I focused on the theological meaning of the story. After the sermon, one well-read elder chastised me for treating the story of Jonah as history. His mind could not let go of the historical-critical issue to listen to what the book of Jonah tells us about God's mercy.

To give myself some credit when I was teaching my Laotian friends about Jesus' stilling of the storm, at least I was trying to avoid the sinkhole of debating the nature and possibility of miracles in the Bible. I can't count the number of sermons I've heard in liberal settings in which the pastor was intent on showing that a biblical miracle could be explained scientifically or rationally—the feeding of the five thousand was not about the miraculous multiplying of loaves and fishes but about the miracle of people sharing with one another; the ailments Jesus healed were not physical but psychosomatic; and so forth.

Fortunately, more and more evangelical scholars and

teachers are returning to a method of interpretation that the earliest Christians used: Christ-centered interpretation. This approach, paradoxically enough, gives us the freedom to read Scripture both historically and critically, and at the right time and place, even therapeutically. That's because the ultimate focus of this method remains on Christ.

The most interesting and persuasive advocate of this reading of Scripture is Hans Boersma. His book *Scripture as Real Presence* describes "real presence" as simply this: "Everything around us is sacramental, in the sense that everything God has created both points to him and makes him present."[2] And then later: "Holy Scripture too is a sacrament, inasmuch as it renders Christ present to us."[3] In other words, no matter where we are in Scripture, it can be a means of encountering Jesus.

He contrasts this with historical exegesis:

> The weakness of historical exegesis, however, is that
> it doesn't treat the Old Testament as a sacrament . . .
> that *already contains* the New Testament reality . . .
> Christ. Or, as Irenaeus and others would have put
> it, strictly historical exegesis doesn't see Christ as the
> treasure hidden in the field of the Old Testament
> (Matt. 13:44) and, therefore, as already really
> present within it.[4]

The argument is more involved and nuanced, but a few examples can help us see the richness of this approach. For example, we can read a passage like Isaiah 7:14—"All right then, the Lord himself will give you the sign. Look! The virgin will conceive a child! She will give birth to a son and will call him Immanuel (which means 'God is with us')"—and not get bogged down debating whether the original Hebrew meant "young woman" or "virgin." We can acknowledge that probably in the original context, Isaiah could only imagine that a young woman could give birth to a son, and that, with a Christ-centered reading of Scripture, Matthew grasped a deeper dimension to the prophecy precisely because of how God revealed himself in and through the Virgin Mary.

Or take Easter Sunday. With many annual or biannual visitors in the congregation, we immediately think our job is to defend the historicity of the resurrection, and so the Easter sermon becomes a rational defense of this, the greatest of all biblical miracles, and the focus of the sermon is on matters historical and rational.

I without a doubt believe in the bodily resurrection of Jesus, and I think a strong historical case can be made for believing it. And yet after we've made our case for the historicity of the resurrection, many listeners shrug and say, "I guess that makes sense," but they don't know what to do with this information. I've run into a large number of people who have no trouble accepting that Jesus rose from the dead and yet have no clue why this event is so revolutionary.

Instead, we would be wise to so emphasize the *meaning* of the resurrection—what it tells us about Jesus Christ, as the biblical writers do—that when people walk out of our Easter sermons, they are wrestling with the lordship of Christ. We should present the meaning of the resurrection so clearly that they will know that if they believe it, they will have to bend the knee, repent, and proclaim that Jesus is Lord. It won't be an interesting intellectual exercise as much as a life-defining moment.

The point is this: the classic Christ-centered reading of Scripture can save us from both narcissism and intellectualism that each in their own way tempt us to put the focus on anything but Christ himself. To be sure, we cannot ignore the historical and literary issues that surround biblical texts. And, in the end, biblical teaching will change how we live. But if we don't read the Bible first and foremost as telling us about who God is and what he has done for us in Christ, we will only perpetuate the horizontal Christianity that has become so characteristic of evangelical faith and that is, really, the end of faith.

CHAPTER 9

AND NOW, THE STAR OF OUR SHOW . . .

HERE IS THE MOST MEMORABLE and least effective sermon illustration I've ever used:

One day my wife and I were arguing about something—the exact subject has long been forgotten. In the course of the argument—probably when she was getting the best of me—I became so frustrated that I hit our dining room wall with my fist. The wall didn't move, of course, but I expected to at least put a hole in the drywall. As fortune would have it, the place I punched with all my force was backed by a two-by-four beam. Let's just say it hurt.

We both fell silent after that, and I set about sweeping up the kitchen and dining room (we were remodeling at the time). It became immediately apparent that there was something wrong with my hand. I could barely hold on to the broom.

My wife noticed that I was in pain and that my hand didn't look right. She gently lifted my hand to look at it. "I think it's broken," she said. "We need to get you to the emergency room." Her diagnosis was soon affirmed by the medical staff at the clinic.

From the point when she looked at my hand, there was no anger, resentment, or moral superiority on her part—all of which would have been justified. She was just concerned about my welfare. She very well knew there was some part of me that was striking out at her when I hit the wall, but instead she focused on the fact that I had vented my anger elsewhere than at her and was in deep pain as a result of my foolishness.

I used this story in a sermon on grace. It was the final illustration, tailored to drive home the truth that God treats us with kindness and grace even when we show ourselves to be hostile and angry, even toward him. I thought it the perfect illustration.

Turns out, very few listeners heard all that. Comments after the service, and for a few weeks running, were of three sorts:

"Thank you for being so vulnerable and sharing that story."

And, in a low voice so no one else could hear, "I've done that but was too afraid to tell anyone."

And of course, "That was so funny!"

No one ever told me that as a result of this illustration they understood God's grace better. No one.

But they understood *me* better. They had learned something about *my* temper. *My* remodeling efforts. About *my* wife and *my* marriage. And they were entertained. By contemporary standards, it was effective: it was riveting; it was funny; listeners remembered it for weeks, even years.

But they remembered the wrong thing. They remembered *me*. They didn't remember anything about God's grace, as far as I could tell. Therefore, I have concluded it was about the worst illustration I could have used.

The problem is this: this type of sermon illustration is the order of the day in evangelical preaching. And it's one reason evangelical preaching is in dire straits.

The sermon is one time in the week when we have the opportunity to hear about something other than ourselves, other than the horizontal. It's when we hear about God and the wonder and mysteries of his love, of what he's done for us in Christ. But more and more, evangelical preaching has become another way we talk about ourselves, and in this case, to learn about the preacher.

Once again, in the interests of identifying with the culture, the entertainment world has become the model here from start to finish. The sermon in many evangelical churches represents a cross between the patter of a stand-up comic and the opening monologues of late-night television. The idea is to be "authentic"—that is, natural and unscripted—and funny to boot.

This, of course, is naive as naive can get because you can

be sure that those opening monologues are hardly unscripted. The patter of the comedian, as well as his or her persona, has been fashioned and sharpened with months or years of practice. Late-night TV hosts and comics are entertaining, no question about that. But they are entertaining precisely because they are anything but authentic. Instead, they are deeply practiced in their profession.

The evangelical sermon mimics all this but without the use of a teleprompter and without repeating the same shtick that has been honed over months of gigs. There are often no podiums or pulpits, no notes, not to mention a sermon manuscript. You can be sure, however, that the preacher has practiced the sermon and memorized the best lines, as well as the right gestures at the right moment—all so that he or she can appear authentic.

It's not just the setting but the content that communicates the most troublesome thing: that the sermon is, in the end, all about the horizontal. Given the length of the sermon and the method of delivery and the very personal illustrations to drive home the message, it all brings an inadvertent focus on the one who is preaching.

Let me emphasize that word *inadvertent*, because I doubt many preachers invest in this style of contemporary preaching to exalt themselves. These men and women love God and strive to make him known. What they don't recognize is that the style they are engaged in thwarts their desires.

Take the method of delivery—often without a pulpit (at best, a transparent lectern), and often by walking back and forth across the stage while preaching, and doing so for thirty to forty-five minutes, at least half if not up to 75 percent of the worship hour. What all this communicates is that the preacher is far and away the most important person in the room. The preacher is the person upon whom we are riveted for the greater part of the service.

I didn't realize how theologically important the traditional pulpit was until I received a comment after one guest sermon I preached. The church's pastoral team liked to preach from the center of the stage and wander back and forth during the sermon—the stand-up comic style. I, however, stood behind the makeshift pulpit, a wooden lectern sitting on a small table. I did so mainly for practical reasons—I'm pretty dependent on notes or a manuscript, and I didn't wander from them.

After the sermon, one man said to me, "Thanks for preaching from the pulpit." When I asked why, he explained, "The pulpit reminds us that the authority of the preacher comes not from the preacher and his personality. The pulpit is a symbol that the sermon derives its authority from the church, which in turn derives its authority from Scripture."

Pondering his comments for weeks afterward, I realized how much a pulpitless sermon, and especially a sermon delivered in stand-up comic style, does an extraordinarily good job of entertaining people and making the preacher, and not the preached Word, the center of attention.

Add to that the problem of content. Make no mistake: Jesus is preached in many evangelical churches still. But not necessarily, and not necessarily foremost.

We evangelicals are suckers for the practical sermon that

tells us how to live for Jesus. But too often, the practical crowds out the biblical. A sermon on "Five Ways to Keep Your Marriage Strong" might mention Jesus or the Bible here and there, but take away those references, and the substance of the sermon remains the same: practical relational psychology. In a similar vein, we might hear sermons on how to manage one's finances with the key insights drawn from financial self-help literature, decorated with verses from Proverbs. And then there are the sermons on raising children and finding a career and working against abortion and so on.

Such sermons are full of sound and wise advice, and we need sound and wise advice on many topics. The question is: Is this the most vital, relevant thing we have to communicate *in worship*? The one time in the week when we gather to praise and glorify the God and Father of our Lord Jesus Christ—is this really the most important thing we can say? Have we exhausted the treasures and wonders of God's Word? Have we said all we can say about the glories of salvation? Or are we bored with talk about God, so that we revert once again to talk about ourselves and how to make our lives more manageable?

One giveaway that we are deeply tempted by the horizontal in our preaching is the number of illustrations preachers use from their own lives. There was a time when preachers were seriously discouraged from using their own lives as sermon illustrations. But sometime in the 1960s, that began to change. The idea was to show listeners that the preacher was no different from the listeners and faced the same challenges, difficulties, and temptations as everyone else. This led to more attentive and appreciative listeners, who now felt they could connect psychologically with their preacher.

Today, it's not uncommon to hear a sermon in which the opening, closing, and key illustration from the sermon's main point is taken from the life and experience of the pastor and his family. Such sermons do a wonderful job of helping listeners connect with the pastor. And pastors keep using them precisely because when people leave the service and shake their hands, they say what a wonderful sermon it was, with comments like, "I love hearing about your family" and "Your kids are so cute" and "I really identify with you."

Really? We want our congregations to identify with *us*? This is precisely the problem with personal illustrations: they inadvertently put the spotlight on the preacher. Within a few months of such preaching, everyone knows the quirks of each member of the pastor's family, the triumphs and failures in key parts of his or her life, the pastor's passions and dislikes, and so forth. In the end, they know more about their pastor than they know about Jesus.

Some pastors defend the practice by saying they use only negative examples of themselves—talking about ways in which they have failed to live up to the call of Christ. What they don't seem to comprehend is that this just raises their status even higher with the congregation. Invariably, the illustrations turn on a moment of realization when the preacher recognized his or her flaw and changed direction. So now the pastor is a model of humility! And even if a pastor says, "I still struggle with this," either no one really believes it, or else they exalt the pastor as a model of spiritual seriousness.

There is, in short, hardly a way to use an illustration from one's personal life without it distracting the listeners' gaze from Jesus, the author and perfecter of our faith. That role has now been subsumed by the preacher, who depends on the personal illustration to make the sermon relevant.

Too many evangelical pastors have become addicted to using personal illustrations because, let's face it, they love the feedback. People pump their hand after the service and tell them how much they enjoyed that little story. I know this firsthand. Pastors are a lonely and insecure lot, and we need affirmation as much as (and maybe more than) everyone else. It is very difficult to resist this temptation in a day when the personal, the intimate, and the tell-all is the order of the day everywhere else.

It is no wonder that we've stopped understanding this part of the service as "worship": it isn't in so many of our churches. In this regard, I thank God for praise choruses— they at least keep the service from completely collapsing into the horizontal.

The way forward is not hard to fathom, and let me take the privilege of being more hortatory in this chapter, as I do have experience in preaching.

First, we might bring back pulpits. They don't have to be the kind that remind us of churches of yesteryear. How about designing a contemporary pulpit that accents that the preacher has been commissioned by the church and that the sermon is finally under the authority of the church—all of which is under the authority of God? Something that says in its design that at this moment, the sermon—the spoken word of God—is not about the speaker of that word but about the God who stands with and above the preacher.

Second, pastors might shorten the sermon so that the service is not dominated by one person and one voice. We can make room for more singing. Make room for more prayer. Make room for silence. Maybe make room for the regular celebration of the sacraments/ordinances. In other words, we can make room for God.

That means congregations have to give the pastor more time for sermon preparation. As hard as it might be to believe, it takes more time to prepare a shorter sermon than a longer one, because every word and phrase becomes more weighted. It requires the preacher to think hard about what to keep in and what to leave out.

Third, I'd suggest preachers put a moratorium on personal illustrations—or at least go to some lengths to curtail the number. Preachers can tell they have become addicted to personal illustrations the moment they decide to stop using them. Try for a few weeks not to use any, and what you'll see is your mind returning to yourself and your experience time and again to drive home a point.

Of course, in a *People* magazine and Facebook culture—where we are dying to know the intimate details of others' lives, where people don't seem authentic unless they reveal something from their personal lives—well, we cannot be effective communicators without dropping in the occasional personal illustration. People want to identify personally with speakers and preachers and writers. So if we want to gain an audience in this culture, we have to offer a bit of ourselves.

This is precisely why, when I am a guest speaker at a church, I try to include one personal illustration toward the beginning of my talk. For better or worse, it makes it more likely that the audience will give me an ear. It's also why my publisher asked me to include a few in this book.

So I get it. But I'm unclear why pastors, who have all sorts of occasions other than worship to let the congregation see them as more than preachers, need week after week to draw on their own lives to drive home a point in sermon after sermon. And I've seen too many instances when the personal anecdote becomes such a crutch that a cult of personality slowly but surely begins to develop around these pastors.

Part of why pastors fall back on personal illustrations is sheer laziness—believe me, I speak from personal acquaintance with the vice. It's so much easier to reach into our memories than it is to read extensively. And when Sunday morning is breathing down our necks, it's just too easy to reach for the personal illustration.

Part of this is due to the fact that preachers do not feel they have time to read widely and deeply in literature, in history, in politics, in theology. So they don't have anything in the tank when they sit down to write a sermon. It's another reason congregations need to insist that their pastors take anywhere from ten to fifteen hours a week in sermon preparation.

Fourth, preachers need to ask themselves at the beginning, the middle, and the end of sermon preparation, *Is this mostly about God? Does this help people better grasp who God is and what he has done for us in Christ? Does it first and foremost exalt Christ?*

One sign of how horizontal our faith has become is the internal objection that our minds raise at this point: *Really? Can I preach about God week after week? I mean, how much can I say about Christ before it gets old or I start repeating myself?*

As if God were finite. As if there were only so much we can say about his countless attributes. As if heaven will get boring after a few weeks of praise because we will have run out of things to praise.

The other objection, of course, is a good one: *Doesn't my congregation need guidance on how to live in Christ?* Yes! And when that guidance is thoroughly and firmly grounded in who Christ is and what he has done for us, then it will be more relevant and meaningful than anything we can conjure up by talking about our needs using the highlight reels from our lives.

CHAPTER 10

MAKING SMALL GROUPS BIGGER IN PURPOSE

ONE OF THE REMARKABLE TRANSFORMATIONS of church life has occurred in my lifetime: the rise of small groups. By this I specifically mean believers gathering regularly in groups of six to twelve to read Scripture or devotional material, to share the arc of their spiritual lives as intimately as trust allows, and to pray together.

This movement began in dribs and drabs in the 1950s and 1960s with a handful of pioneering efforts. The one I was most familiar with was Faith at Work, whose leaders Bruce Larson and Keith Miller, among others, helped lead the way. This short-lived organization looked back to the work of Sam Shoemaker, an Episcopal priest who put Alcoholics Anonymous on the map for churches. AA was the original inspiration for small groups in churches, where the emphasis was on members sharing their struggles in order to receive support and encouragement from one another.

My mother was a local Faith at Work leader, and I still remember the challenges and exhilaration that such groups experienced. The challenges usually had to do with people who attended a small group but were afraid to open up about their struggles. They had been schooled to believe that the Christian life was always a victorious one. To reveal a weakness or doubt or struggle was not a sign of honesty but of a lack of faith.

The exhilaration was due to the fact that many Christians in devout churches felt free for the first time to acknowledge what was really going on with them and found other Christians with whom they could honestly share their experiences without judgment. The testimony times at Faith at Work regional conferences were tear-filled events as people basked in their freedom to be frank about their spiritual lives.

Starting in earnest in the 1970s, evangelical churches began seeing the value of small groups, in large part due to another pioneer, Lyman Coleman. Ironically, the explosion of megachurches increased the demand for small groups. Pastors of churches with two thousand or more attending quickly realized they had to supplement Sunday morning worship with a vehicle to get people to know one another better.

Today, small groups are ubiquitous in the church. You know they have become an institution when scholars start studying them. James Bielo's *Words Upon the Word* is a fascinating ethnographic study of small-group Bible studies. He summarized the scholarly interest at the beginning of his 2009 book. After listing a few analyses by sociologist Robert Wuthnow, he says,

> Wuthnow argues that, beginning in the 1960s, Americans have steadily rearranged their search for community belonging, seeking small group opportunities in place of larger, more formal institutional structures. Among these, small group Bible study is the most prolific in American life, with more than 30 million men and women participating in these groups at least once a week. This bears repeating: no other form of small group, religious or otherwise, is as widespread in American life as group Bible study.[1]

Given the theme of this book—the call for us to love God with all our heart, soul, mind, and strength—I naturally have given a lot of thought to the small group phenomenon, which has now become the main vehicle by which Christians read their Bible and grow in their faith. Small group ministries are some of the most dynamic in the contemporary church, and so, as small group leaders know all too well, they are full of opportunities for spiritual blessing and curse. The challenges are best addressed by others called more deeply into this form of ministry. Here I want to think about them from the angle that is driving this book: how they encourage the horizontal at the expense of the vertical.

If we believe small groups are first and foremost an intimate setting to grow in our understanding of Scripture and our maturity in Christ with others, we have to acknowledge the ways they are and are not succeeding. We have to pull together three megatrends of the last few decades to see the challenge.

One, as noted, is the explosion of small groups in churches since the 1970s.

The second megatrend is the multiplication of Bible translations. Starting with J. B. Phillips's *The New Testament in Modern English*, and followed by *The Living Bible* and *Good News for Modern Man*, there has been a concerted attempt by evangelical publishing houses to produce Bibles that are understandable to the common reader. The problem they are addressing is that fewer and fewer people are reading their Bibles, many saying they don't read the Bible because it is too hard to understand. Their solution is to make the Bible easier to read. And so we've seen the appearance of the New King James Version, the New International Version, the English Standard Version, the New Living Translation, and the Message, among others.

The third megatrend is—according to studies by Pew, Gallup, Lifeway, and Barna—that Americans in general and Christians in particular are more biblically illiterate than ever. We struggle to name the four Gospels, let alone the Ten Commandments; we can't discern the difference between Old Testament and New Testament stories or their chronological order; and we think nonbiblical quotes (like "God helps those who help themselves") are in Scripture. Professors at Christian colleges increasingly complain at how much remedial Bible work they have to do with today's incoming freshmen.

These trends come together in this way: the decline in biblical literacy has occurred during the same period when Bible translations were modernized and small group Bible studies blossomed. It appears that the two leading strategies to encourage Bible engagement have failed.

To be sure, such large-scale phenomena cannot so facilely be related like this, but it does give one pause for thought. And one could argue that if it weren't for new Bible translations and small group ministries, things would be much worse on the Bible literacy front. That very well could be. But I suspect the problem may lie deeper, which suggests how small group ministries in particular might adapt.

INTIMACY HUMAN AND DIVINE

The need for smaller fellowships is felt more deeply than ever. One megatrend that has encouraged their growth is the rapid expansion of mass society. Starting with industrialization, our culture has become increasingly large-scale and impersonal. Instead of the small schoolhouse of mixed ages, we now attend primary, middle, and secondary schools divided precisely into twelve grades, with some high schools having more than eight thousand students.[2] A typical major university today can have more than fifty thousand students, with the University of Central Florida having the largest enrollment in recent years, topping off at 68,571 in 2018–19.[3]

Few of us today work in family-centered industries but in huge national and global enterprises, like Exxon and Wells Fargo and Apple and Microsoft and hundreds of other transnational companies. Our yearning for "economies of scale" has been a key ideal in the growth of megachurches and multisite churches.

It has taken churches a bit longer than the rest of society to feel the strain of impersonal culture because well into the twentieth century churches remained the center of social life for most Americans. But increasingly men and women of the twentieth century found the church less and less meaningful and began to drift away. Churches began to see the small group as a way to reverse this trend.

One small group leader described in a blog post how Lyman Coleman understood the purpose of small groups and how churches adapted this concept to their needs:

> "In the early days," Lyman says, "the small group movement was primarily an underground movement. The established church didn't want anything to do with it." Later, churches began to recognize small groups as "the best way of reaching out beyond the doors of the church to the broken people in our society." Coleman has always wanted small groups to be places for caring and deep relationships, where people can belong and feel wanted, and he believes that healthy groups can have the effect of helping to close the back door of a church, but he bristles at small groups being purely an assimilation strategy.

His feelings are deep and very personal. "Every time
in my life," he said in 1992, "at times of my deepest
needs, my needs were not on the church's agenda."
His sentiment should continue to convict us as
leaders today.[4]

So although Coleman started small groups with no ulterior motive but to bring people together in a more intimate
setting, churches began to see their utility at attracting and
keeping people in church. In either case, we have to note the
driving emotional force of small groups: "caring and deep
relationships, where people can belong and feel wanted."

This is the genius of small groups. Given the increasing
alienation that mass society brings, people need places where
they can experience deep relationships and feel connected.
This is one of the blessings of a small group I belong to. The
challenge is figuring out how to prevent this righteous desire
from becoming an idol.

One part of the challenge is the threat of group narcissism:
I reveal a little bit of myself so that you will be encouraged
to reveal a little bit of yourself, and thus the circle continues
until we develop a deeper level of intimacy. It is a powerful
experience to be in a group that grows to deeper and deeper
levels of intimacy—so much so that intimacy can become
an end in itself. This, of course, is just a form of mutual
self-centeredness—a horizontal focus at perhaps its most
dangerous. Why? Because we believe we are deepening our
faith in God, but we are actually just enjoying a mutual back-
scratching. Let me be clear: it is wonderful to find friends

with whom we can share deep and personal matters. That's Christian fellowship at its finest. And yes, we can experience God's presence when we are in the presence of others—Jesus said he would be with any two or three who are gathered in his name. But I'm also aware in my own journey of how the power of mutual intimacy, instead of revealing God in our midst, becomes just a group of like-minded friends.

Some groups check this by making sure the group has a mission outside of themselves. For example, there are some fellowships that, in addition to studying, sharing, and praying with one another, work together on a task: the group runs a food closet or tutors disadvantaged students or rehabs homes in poor neighborhoods. Anyone who has experienced this type of small group knows how powerfully people bond with one another when they are engaged in a common mission outside themselves. Along the way, of course, they begin to discover some of the intimate details of others' lives as they work together—a wonderful by-product of outward-focused small groups.

In addition, this sort of group involves being discipled in the art of loving others. One reason we love the traditional small group model is that we naturally feel comfortable meeting people like ourselves, who come from our same social, economic, and class spheres. It's one reason we rarely if ever find traditional, community-focused small groups that span social classes. But in small groups that reach out to others, they often end up reaching out to people very unlike the members of the group (often poorer, of a different ethnic or racial group, and so forth). Add to that the need to minister to one another as they together confront challenges and obstacles to the mission. The main purpose of the group stretches beyond the experience of homogeneous community.

Beyond group narcissism, there is one significant challenge of the now traditional way that some do small groups: despite members' good intentions, small groups often are unable to ground members ever deeper into Scripture.

A friend wrote a blog post a few years ago about biblical illiteracy in the church. He described the problem in a little detail, and his solution was that small groups would help churchgoers better study and understand Scripture. I think he was wrong on two counts. First, as noted above, during the rise of the small group movement, biblical illiteracy has only increased. So while some small groups may in fact increase biblical literacy here and there, as a whole they don't seem to be doing the job.

Second, and more to the point, is the psychological reality of small groups. It is common for small groups that started off studying the Bible to sooner or later move away from studying the Bible. Why is that?

First, because studying the Bible—understanding the original context, making theological connections, and then seeing how all that applies to the lives of group members—is hard work. Studying the Bible requires a fairly high level of intellectual energy.

How much easier it is to read together a book by Max Lucado or watch a video by Beth Moore. They explain all the hard stuff and do so in a way that is entertaining and inspiring. Let me be clear: I am a fan of Max Lucado and

Beth Moore. These two are among many others who have become popular teachers in evangelical life for good reason. Many gifted teachers have produced books and videos that attempt to help small groups grow deeper in their faith. I daresay all of them would insist that, when push comes to shove, people ought to be spending more time in the Bible than listening to them.

One can welcome the occasional use of such videos in small groups while recognizing the problem of depending on them. When we listen to the wonderful insights and gripping stories that the Bible teachers offer, we're enthralled. Yet when we ourselves read the Bible, we seem incapable of coming up with those insights and relating them to our own lives. And so, instead of such videos encouraging us to get into Scripture, they mostly encourage us to buy another book or video series.

Yet even when small groups manage to eschew mutual narcissism and encourage Bible literacy and growth in Christ, the overall emphasis still seems to be horizontal. Small groups are by their very nature driven by horizontal concerns—intimate relationships with others and concern for the state of members' souls.

We need small groups to help us learn to love one another in the church and to help us think more deeply about the state of our souls. Some small groups would do well to give greater attention to the vertical. That means incorporating a third dimension to the group: not just mutual intimacy, not just moral growth, but also deepening a yearning and love for God. Perhaps some meetings could be devoted to prayer, including lots of room for silence. We're usually uncomfortable when there is too much silence in group prayer, but if it was announced ahead of time that the silence is an opportunity to listen to God, it would free people from wanting to fill the silence. Or a group could do a series on how to praise and glorify God in prayer and in our lives or read a book on Christian meditation and contemplative prayer. Just punctuating the usual small group routine with meetings that force the focus on God and away from ourselves can make a remarkable difference.

Adding this third dimension would almost automatically check the temptation of mutual narcissism. It would also ignite a greater interest and passion for reading Scripture.

My sense is that lack of interest in the Bible today is not driven by the Bible's difficulty. Yes, that is something that needs to be attended to. But I believe at our core, we don't like reading the Bible because we don't love God, and don't want to love him, as much as we say we do. We don't yearn for him, long for him, wish to hear him speak to us. I'll elaborate on this in future chapters. The point here is that if yearning for God becomes one of the purposes of small groups then I believe that studying the Bible will be energized in dynamic ways, and understanding the Word of God will grow by leaps and bounds.

———

Part 2 was about the church, from the very way we conceive of it to how we live out church life in our day. I've pointed out how we are sorely tempted by the horizontal in every aspect of the church's life. Our horizontal myopia is a serious problem for each and every one of us. At the same time, I trust I have written in a way that communicates that we should be as compassionate with ourselves as God is with us. We all struggle mightily to put God first, to make him our all in all, because we are sinful and self-centered, yes, and also because we are weak and needy.

The way forward is not easy. It is more complex than we might at first imagine. And yet, there definitely is a way forward—or better, upward.

PART 3

DEEPENING DESIRE

CHAPTER 11

SHAPING DESIRE

I BEGAN THIS BOOK by reminding us how the passion for knowing and loving God is what drives the psalmists, the prophets, and Paul, to name three examples from Scripture. I also noted how this passion is expressed by various saints in the history of the church. This—a desire for God, a yearning to see his face—is the pinnacle of the Christian life now and in the hereafter.

I then examined US evangelical Christianity and argued that while a passion for God was evident in the earliest years of the movement, as time progressed, our focus has become increasingly horizontal.

Part 2 looked at how aspects of the church have been co-opted by the horizontal—from our very understanding of the church itself to worship to preaching to small groups.

Simply put, we have been created to love and adore God above all else. Evangelical Christians in particular have a unique legacy of adoring God. But we have largely forgotten God and replaced him with a variety of causes, stances, and ways of thinking and acting that focus our desires at the level of the horizontal. This is not to deny that a passion for God remains in many sectors of evangelical life—it surely does. But I think it's fair to say that we are no longer a people who are *characterized* by a hunger and thirst to know God.

The question is, of course, can we change what we desire? I've argued that we have misplaced desires, either focused on the self or focused on human flourishing as such. I've argued that our desire should first and foremost be for God with the assumption that, yes, all these other things will be added unto us—but only if we keep our desires in order.

Some instinctively respond, "No—you either have the desire for something or you don't. It's something wired into us." And so they read what I've said and conclude, "I guess I'm not a very good Christian" or "Maybe I'm not even a Christian, because I certainly don't have the desire for God that the biblical and historical saints did."

Some have given up on faith precisely for this reason: they simply admitted they didn't care all that much about God. If others want to pursue faith, all well and good—let them follow their bliss. But as for me and my house, we will ignore religion.

I will admit that this view—that specific desires are wired into us—has held me in its grip for most of my life. In retrospect, this has led to problems I won't go into here. Suffice it to say, my thinking turned after reading about desire in a different context: technology.

WHY DO WE LOVE TECHNOLOGY?

Like many others, I have become increasingly aware of how contemporary media technology manipulates us—or, more to the point, how it manipulates our desires. This was one theme in Jacob Weisberg's *New York Review of Books* essay "We Are Hopelessly Hooked," from which the following insights are gleaned.[1]

He notes, for example, that the Persuasive Technology Lab at Stanford, a branch of the university's Human Sciences and Technologies Advanced Research Institute, has produced "some of Silicon Valley's most successful app designers" today. One prominent professor, B. J. Fogg, who founded the lab in 1998, also runs "persuasion boot camps" for tech companies.

"He . . . [teaches the] discipline of capturing people's attention and making it hard for them to escape," says Weisberg. "Fogg's behavior model involves building habits through the use of what he calls 'hot triggers,' like the links and photos in Facebook's newsfeed, made up largely of posts by one's Facebook friends."

One of Fogg's students, Nir Eyal, offers up concrete suggestions for how to do this in *Hooked: How to Build Habit-Forming Products*. A successful app is one that "creates a 'persistent routine' or behavioral loop," summarizes Weisberg. "The app both triggers a need and provides the momentary solution to it." He then quotes Eyal:

Feelings of boredom, loneliness, frustration,
confusion, and indecisiveness often instigate a
slight pain or irritation and prompt an almost
instantaneous and often mindless action to quell
the negative sensation. . . . Gradually, these bonds
cement into a habit as users turn to your product
when experiencing certain internal triggers.

Take the Facebook trigger called FOMO, the fear of missing out. The social network both creates in us anxiety when we're away from it and satisfies that craving with a sense of connection to others when we return, which in one sense validates us. On Facebook, the number of likes, friends, and comments cements our social status. According to Eyal, checking in delivers a hit of dopamine to the brain along with the craving for another hit.

Sound familiar? This is basic slot-machine psychology applied to social media. Eyal believes Instagram does all this in spades, raising the ante from fear of missing out to fear of missing that special moment.

Sherry Turkle, in her bestselling *Reclaiming Conversation: The Power of Talk in a Digital Age*, describes how people talk about their use of social media. When trying to cut down on their social media usage, they instinctively describe their experience in the language of substance abuse. They say they are "hooked" or "addicted" to social media, and the days and weeks they leave it are "detoxing" or "going cold turkey."[2]

In other words, it's not an accident that social media is

all-consuming and addictive. It's deliberately designed that way by its creators and managers. They create triggers that manipulate—that is, *change*—our desires.

This is something marketers have been doing successfully for a century or more: they work to get us to desire a product so that we buy it. They do that with various means, from showing how a product solves a problem to convincing us that it is cool to own the product—and dozens of techniques between. We all recognize how we have been and are willingly manipulated by marketers, especially when it comes to the cool factor.

This is one of the greatest draws of Apple's products. It would be hard to argue that the iPhone is head-and-shoulders superior in quality to other phones, but many of us own them because, well, we think they are the coolest smartphones. They are a status marker. Walk into a business meeting at which everyone brings their laptops, and there is an unspoken assumption that the Macs are the coolest in the room. We've drunk the "cool-aid" (forgive the pun).

The point is, every day we recognize that our desires can be shaped and manipulated by app designers and marketers. That leads me to conclude that perhaps my own desires can be shaped, that there may be means by which I can become hungrier for God.

In *The Atlantic*, Olga Khazan drives home this point in "'Find Your Passion' Is Awful Advice."[3] She begins with an anecdote that suggests the problem: Carol Dweck, a psychology professor at Stanford University, asked a group of undergraduate students, "How many of you are waiting to find your passion?"

"Almost all of them raised their hand and got dreamy looks in their eyes," Dweck said. When she asked them to explain, they described it as if a "tidal wave [of desire] would sweep over them" and that this was the sort of thing that would be enough to motivate them for their whole careers.

What Dweck said next is what Khazan explains at length in the article: "I hate to burst your balloon, but it doesn't usually happen that way."

Not only that, but believing this is a good way to remain aimless for a long, long time. Paul O'Keefe, assistant professor of psychology at Yale–NUS College, put it this way: "That means that if you do something that feels like work, it means you don't love it." Take for example the student who tries to find a research topic that arouses her intellectual passion by moving from lab to lab. "It's this idea," said O'Keefe, "that if I'm not completely overwhelmed by emotion when I walk into a lab, then it won't be my passion or my interest."

Dweck and her Stanford colleague Greg Walton recently performed a study that suggests passions aren't found but instead are developed.

Walton says the idea of finding a passion and then responding to it "doesn't reflect the way I or my students experience school, where you go to a class and have a lecture or a conversation, and you think, *That's interesting.* It's through a process of investment and development that you develop an abiding passion in a field."

In other words, our passions are formed as we give

ourselves wholeheartedly to something. And that means sticking with something through the inevitable periods of boredom and dreariness that accompany any activity after a while. If we do that, slowly but surely our interest in and even fascination with a subject grows.

This doesn't mean we can become equally passionate about every single thing we pursue. It does mean we can become passionate about anything we believe we should be passionate about—*especially if that passion coincides with basic human nature.*

I don't want to get into a debate about whether anyone who wants to can become equally passionate about playing chess or designing dresses. We stand on firmer ground, however, when we insist that if a person wants to become passionate about knowing and loving God, then deepening that desire is possible and doable. God, president of his own Persuasive Technology Company, is the one who gives us the means to do just that.

Why can I assert that in an unqualified way? For one, because knowing and loving God is fundamental to human nature. "Our hearts are restless until they rest in Thee" is how Augustine put it. Christian theology recognizes that we were created to be in loving relationship with our Creator. Though that intent has been thwarted by sin, it remains the deepest and most fundamental desire of the human heart. In our broken state, it often comes disguised as an attraction to fine art or music, to deep poetry, to exquisite foods, to the intimacies of sexual love. Such things prompt our hearts and minds toward the transcendent, and their work as pointers

only becomes clear when we give ourselves to their Author
and Sustainer.

If this is what we were ultimately made for—to know,
love, and glorify God and enjoy him forever—then it seems
fair to conclude that God will make it possible for us to pursue him. And in fact, he has.

This does not mean that we can by our own efforts attain
God's forgiveness and salvation, that by our own efforts we
can manipulate our desires. First, the assumption here is that
we have already been saved by grace and that this is not our
own doing. This book is not about earning salvation but
about how to live and move and have our being once we have
been saved. And I'm not arguing that though we are saved by
grace, we now grow by works. That's not only theologically
ridiculous but also does not match the experience of those
who have grown in Christ. They are the first to say it is grace
first and last.

But it's just as ridiculous to imagine ourselves as completely passive in this process. There are things we *do*. But
our doing is not about striving to be accepted. We have not
only made the team; we are in the starting lineup. The passion that drives us is not fear or anxiety but the desire to excel
on the field of play.

We also have to acknowledge how God's grace has begun
this whole process. He has implanted in every human heart
a desire for him. He has graced some to know that their
various horizontal desires are merely pointers to him. The
fact that we might want to read such a book as this and
think about increasing desire for God is evidence of God

already working in our hearts, minds, and souls to deepen our love for him. That desire to desire God is in fact a divine gift.

Before I get into specifics as to what this looks like—that is, how exactly do we deepen our desire for God?—let me be clear. This is not easy. I'm not writing as someone who has reached this mountaintop. I fail more days than I succeed. And I think that is the way with this desire. It goes against nearly everything we're accustomed to. It goes against all those natural desires that lead us by the nose day-to-day. It fights with all the fear and anger that go hand in hand with a relationship with God. It's the hardest thing we can pursue, especially because there is an enemy who works night and day to sabotage our efforts.

So it's not simply a matter of willfully committing to pursue God. It is that, but that very will is subject to ebbs and flows—some victories, to be sure, but also many defeats. And that will is deeply conflicted. My usual prayer in this matter is not "Lord, help me see you more clearly and love you more dearly," but often two steps back: "Lord, I confess today that I really don't want to love you. Help me to want to desire you more than anything."

One classic prayer that gets to the heart of our confusion and rebellion and plain self-centeredness is called the Litany of Humility. It has been attributed to Rafael Cardinal Merry del Val (1865–1930), but the structure has a history. The version attributed to him is used by many today to get at the many desires that lie in our breasts, the ones that get in the way of the greatest desire we long to know:

O Jesus. Meek and humble of heart, Hear me.
From the desire of being esteemed, Deliver me, Jesus.
From the desire of being loved, Deliver me, Jesus.
From the desire of being extolled, . . .
From the desire of being honored, . . .
From the desire of being praised, . . .
From the desire of being preferred to others, . . .
From the desire of being consulted, . . .
From the desire of being approved, . . .
From the fear of being humiliated, . . .
From the fear of being despised, . . .
From the fear of suffering rebukes, . . .
From the fear of being calumniated, . . .
From the fear of being forgotten, . . .
From the fear of being ridiculed, . . .
From the fear of being wronged, . . .
From the fear of being suspected, . . .
That others may be loved more than I,
    Jesus, grant me the grace to desire it.
That others may be esteemed more than I, . . .
That, in the opinion of the world, others may increase
    and I may decrease, . . .
That others may be chosen and I set aside, . . .
That others may be praised and I unnoticed, . . .
That others may be preferred to me in everything, . . .
That others may become holier than I, provided that
    I may become as holy as I should, Jesus, grant me
    the grace to desire it.[4]

This whole prayer is premised on one underlying desire: to know and love God. And the petition for that is the same as for the others: "Grant me the grace to desire it."

Again, we must acknowledge the mystery and complexity of desire. I can say, "I don't feel like loving God right now, let alone doing what he commands," and at the same time say, "But that's what I really want." Or to put it another way, my mind and will have chosen to love God with every part of my being, but parts of my being—the heart, at least—are not following suit.

Start talking about this philosophically, and things get even more complex. Desire is not a simple thing, and fueling it is not as simple as manipulating social media desires. It is only by God's grace that we even want to begin this journey, and it is only by God's grace that we'll make any progress.

This entire book, in fact, is founded on a truth that is greater and more important than the theme of this book. We may have forgotten God, but he has not forgotten us. And he not only urges and prompts us to remember him, but he gives us the means of grace to do just that.

CHAPTER 12

LOVE AND LOATHING

THE WRITER OF PROVERBS SAYS THAT "fear of the LORD is the beginning of wisdom" (9:10, NRSV). The fear he refers to is a healthy reverence and awe. But there is another type of fear we have to wrestle with in our relationship with God. In terms of that fear, I'd put it like this: the fear of God is the beginning of longing for him.

I ended the last chapter noting that we do in fact long to know and love God at some deep level. We do desire God. In spite of all the ways we have forgotten him—that is, marginalized God in our flurry of horizontal activity—we still want God. Does this contradict what I've been arguing? Not really.

I have drawn a stark contrast between the vertical and horizontal dimensions of faith to bring some clarity and urgency to the problem. Such stark contrast is hyperbole designed to drive home a point. But if I were to turn now and say all we have to do is make up our minds to start desiring God, I will have moved from hyperbole to fiction. It's not that simple.

Deep down we still desire God, despite all the focus on the horizontal. And yet the reason for the horizontal focus is not just that we have forgotten God—as if we just got distracted, like going to the store to buy milk, filling the shopping cart, and going home without what we came for. No, we have forgotten God because we deliberately try to erase him from our memory. That's because sometimes God is like a bad dream that leaves us confused and anxious.

It is crucial that we see and recognize this dimension of our relationship with God. If God doesn't at times leave us confused and anxious, we have not yet met the living God.

Just ask Abraham, who could not for his life figure out how God was going to produce a great nation from his aged loins.

Ask Jacob, who is said to have wrestled with God and lost.

Ask Moses, whose whole purpose in life was to lead the people of Israel into the Promised Land, only to be denied entry himself.

Ask David, who in many psalms complained that the Lord did not hear him.

Ask Jeremiah, who was furious with God for prodding him to preach.

Ask Jesus, who felt as if God had forsaken him on the cross.

Every believer sooner or later knows it is a fearsome thing

to fall into the hands of this God. Which is why any believer worth his or her salt is deeply ambivalent about God. Yes, we yearn to be ruled by Unfailing Wisdom—and yet we resent having to submit to anyone or anything. We crave intimacy with Pure Benevolence—but we fear the loss of independence. We resent the one we long for, and we are afraid of the one we desire. In short, we love God and we hate God.

We can make no progress in the spiritual life until we acknowledge this. If we think we really do love God, and all we need is a gentle reminder to put him back on the throne of our lives, we're kidding ourselves. We're living a fantasy faith. That is simply not the sordid and splendid reality of the human heart.

One large reason we resent God and would just as soon forget about him is that he refuses to come to us in the way we think we need him to come to us. We reason like this: God is magnificent and wondrous and knows no limits; thus he will come to us in unmistakable splendor. Yet our prayers waft into the silent beyond. Worship feels like a mud puddle of words. We ask for healing, and we end up paying medical bills. We long for love and file for divorce. Where is the God of miracle and wonder when we need him? He does not seem very dependable. And rather than look to him and be, disappointed time and again, we decide to forget the vertical and focus on the horizontal. We're sensible enough not to abandon Christian faith altogether because in spite of our confusion, we still believe it is the way to eternal life. Just don't ask us to take seriously the presence of God. Maybe the glorious God shows up in other people's lives. Maybe back in the Bible days. Maybe once in our life a long, long time ago. But not today, not here, not in the foreseeable future.

The God of miracle and wonder, of course, is in large part a figment of our imagination. It's the way we want God to be. It's not the way he is day-to-day, eternity to eternity.

No question about it, there are miracles and wonders in the Bible, and some have experienced the power and the glory of God today. But these miracles are not nearly as obvious or as definitive as we sometimes think. Remember that many saw and heard the resurrected Lord right before their very eyes and ears, and yet they still doubted (see Matthew 28:17).

We are wiser to think of miracles and wonder as God's defibrillator. We are sometimes so dead to God that we need an electric shock to the heart to wake us up. But after that, things return to normal, and God returns to his normal mode of address. Man does not live by divine defibrillator alone, for a life of miracles and wonder would kill us. Instead, God comes to us as silently and subtly as the steady beating of our hearts.

If the first step in desiring God is to recognize how much we resent his presence, the second step is to accept the way in which he has chosen to be with us. We have to know what it is we desire. If we desire miracles, we will never find God. If we desire God, we must give up miracles and look for him in the mundane.

Like the human and inadequate words of a preacher.
Like the confusing language and idioms of the Bible.
Like the bread and wine of Communion.
Like the water of baptism.

Like the gathering of two or three coming together for prayer.

Like the everyday experience of mystery, of not knowing, of wonder, of the perplexing—of which life is chock full.

If we look for God in any place but the mundane, we will not find him.

CHAPTER 13

THE WORLD, THE FLESH, THE DEVIL, AND RELIGION

WE NEED TO THINK MORE about how much we resent God, because the more we make God the center of our emotional attention, the more a battle will rage in our hearts. "It is a fearful thing to fall into the hands of the living God" (Hebrews 10:31, NRSV), and it is a trying thing to wish to love God with heart, soul, mind, and strength.

When we yearn to yearn for God, certain realities join forces to thwart us. Traditionally, they've been summarized as the world, the flesh, and the devil. This is an awfully good summary, to which I would add just one more: religion. In this chapter, we will look at each of these in Luke's order of the temptations of Jesus in the wilderness (4:3-13).

THE DEVIL

We are wise neither to ignore nor to spend excessive time on this theme. As C. S. Lewis noted in his preface to *The Screwtape Letters,*

> There are two equal and opposite errors into which our race can fall about the devils. One is to disbelieve in their existence. The other is to believe, and to feel an excessive and unhealthy interest in them. They themselves are equally pleased by both errors and hail a materialist or a magician with the same delight.[1]

If one does want to spend a bit of time pondering "the wiles of the devil," Lewis's classic is the place to go. For our purposes here, I simply note the reality of dark spiritual forces who are dedicated enemies of God.

The origin of such beings, their exact nature, why God would allow them to exist, and other such questions cannot be answered definitively. The Bible is not concerned with the ontology of evil spirits but only recognizes their existence and their power—and their defeat in Christ.

Their existence is taken for granted by Jesus, Paul, John, and all the New Testament writers. Their purpose seems to be to wreak havoc on human life, especially when that life is journeying toward God. They tempt us to abandon God as the devil tempted Jesus to do the same. For some, the devil has made an appearance in sight or smell or sound. For most of us, he makes an appearance in our minds with thoughts that are designed to undermine our love for God and our obedience to him.

Not every such thought is from the enemy. Again, we are not asked to discern the exact nature or whereabouts or methods of the devil. We don't have to ascribe every evil thought to his credit to know that he "prowls about . . . looking for someone to devour," sometimes explicitly "roaring [like a] lion" (1 Peter 5:8) but most often on cat paws so that we are hardly aware of his presence.

So as you become more serious in your desire to love God, do not be surprised if you find yourself assaulted with all manner of temptations or your besetting sins become more tempting still. The very presence of such temptations suggests you are on the right path.

The first order of defense, as always, is prayer. Catholics have a prayer just to this end:

Saint Michael the Archangel,
defend us in battle.
Be our defense against the wickedness
and snares of the Devil.
May God rebuke him, we humbly pray,
and do thou,
O Prince of the heavenly hosts,
by the power of God,
thrust into hell Satan,
and all the evil spirits,
who prowl about the world
seeking the ruin of souls. Amen.[2]

When Protestants suspect that something external may be tempting them, they will want to pray to their Lord along just these lines. And with that, let's forget about the devil and move on to consider aspects of temptation that our minds are capable of grasping.

THE FLESH

The first enticement in Luke's temptation account is this: the devil approaches a very hungry Jesus (who has been fasting for forty days) and says, "If you are the Son of God, tell this stone to become a loaf of bread" (4:3).

The interesting and very wicked thing about this temptation is that it is an attack on something that is fundamentally good. "God looked over all he had made"—including the flesh of animals and man, including the grain that would be used to make bread—"and he saw that it was very good!" (Genesis 1:31). We rejoice and thank God for our bodies, which need to be fed. We thank God for our food, which feeds our good bodies.

The three principal temptations of the flesh are all about desiring good things but seeking them in excessive or inappropriate ways. They amount to greed, gluttony, and lust.

In our time, we are certainly aware of how powerful greed is, though we normally call it materialism. And while we are keenly aware of the tentacles of such temptation, few of us (myself included) do anything significant about it. We may say we don't own our possessions but are merely stewards of the gifts of God, but in our more lucid moments, we know that we are possessed by them and use them mostly for our own selfish ends.

Not that it's as easy as giving them all away on the spur of the moment, like St. Anthony did before he took off for the desert. But the simple fact is that, year after year after year, we cannot keep our accumulation in check—evidenced by the increasing size of the homes we need to store all our stuff. We lament this, and yet we seem incapable of actually turning this around.

Simply put, if we don't get a handle on this inordinate love of the flesh, we will not be able to make room in our little hearts to love God with all of them.

In a similar vein, we have to acknowledge how prevalent the sin of gluttony is, at least in America today. Setting aside those who have medical conditions that cause their bodies to swell with fat at the slightest intake of food, for the rest of us, it's a simple matter of gluttony. We are not to judge others as we scan their waistlines—God knows what's going on; we don't have to know. And of course, there is no one ideal body type; God forbid we hold up thinness as a new idol.

But come on, now. There comes a point when we need to be honest with ourselves and recognize that we have, indeed, been living gluttonously. Those of us who have fought this temptation our whole adult lives (present company included) would do well to stop cursing our belt notches when we gain another and bless God for this, because few sins have such an outward and visible sign of an inward and invisible greed. It is a physical sign of a broken spiritual reality.

But gluttony can be invisible, as well. For gluttony is

not overeating as much as it is an inordinate and spiritually unhealthy focus on food and health. Many friends who have no problem maintaining their weight and working out admit they spend way too much time thinking about such matters. So let us overeaters not fall into envy over the slim and trim, and let not the slim and trim judge those with expanding waistlines. Let us be generous with one another, recognizing that most of us struggle with gluttony at least now and again and that gluttony is a very difficult sin to abandon.

Finally, there is sexual lust. In my view, traditional Christians spend too much time worrying about the sin of homosexual relations and not enough about the lusts that are much more prevalent among them, namely extramarital affairs and especially our addiction to pornography and masturbation. Without giving homosexual relations and extramarital affairs a pass, we need to address this latter plague especially.

We are rife with statistics about the problem, but the numbers vary. One reason is that pornography is not easily defined. Regardless, none of the statistics are encouraging. Let's just talk about a Barna study from a couple of years ago.[3] According to the study, more than half of pastors (57 percent) and nearly two-thirds of youth pastors (64 percent) have struggled with porn at one time or another. And when it comes to the general population, 67 percent of teen and young adult men and 33 percent of teen and young adult women seek out porn at least monthly. The numbers go down for older men and women, but not by much. And there is reason to believe the numbers are comparable in the Christian community.

Masturbation has become more acceptable than it used to be in the Christian community, especially among young people. It is certainly not the worst sin in the world, and self-satisfaction is no reason for self-loathing. But it is the very nature of masturbation to use one's sexuality to satisfy one's own desires, when sex has explicitly been designed by God for sharing with another. Thus, by its very nature, it thwarts love. This is not good for human relationships, and it is not good if we are trying to make more room in our hearts for God. If we cannot love God and mammon, even less can we love God and masturbation.

It's fair to say that many of those reading this book are struggling or have struggled with porn and masturbation, and this author is no exception. This is no time for us men especially to pretend this isn't a temptation or that, given the ease with which technology makes porn available, it is going away any time soon. The good news is that, with God's help, this too can be cast out, as many can attest.

These temptations of the flesh don't attack us individually but usually work in concert. It's not unusual to be fighting the temptation to view pornography while struggling with gluttony and materialism. So don't be surprised that when you succumb to one, you'll succumb to the others. It's often a package deal, and it's why spiritual writers lump them all together under one term: the flesh.

It's also why the three principal monastic vows have been chastity, poverty, and obedience. Chastity aims at lust, poverty at greed and gluttony, and obedience at "the flesh" that wants what it wants when it wants it. While Protestants will not enter the monastic life, we can practice one discipline that has shown itself to be extraordinarily successful at disciplining the flesh: fasting.

And I mean fasting from food. We commonly hear about people fasting from all manner of things today, but there are theological and spiritual reasons the church has focused on food. After all, the first sin was lusting after food. It is somehow core to the human dilemma: we absolutely need food to survive, and yet food can be our spiritual downfall. Since all sins of the flesh are closely related, if we can learn to discipline desires in regard to food, discipline in other areas will more likely follow suit.

What fasting teaches us is to live with unfulfilled desire. If we cannot learn that in regard to desires of the flesh, we will struggle when it comes to the spiritual desires of the heart. To embark on the journey to behold the face of God is to embark on a journey of unfulfilled desire. We will more and more find ourselves enraptured in his love *and at the same time* longing for more of it. And given that we are finite and God is infinite, there will never come a time when we are completely satisfied and satiated with the love of God. We have to get used to living with unfulfilled desire if we are to grasp what the love of God entails.

In another sense, fasting makes our hearts larger and larger, clearing out inappropriate loves and creating more room for the love of God to inhabit. It should not surprise us, then, that this is just the time when temptation will make itself felt more powerfully than ever—just as it did for Jesus during his fast in the wilderness.

As serious as sins of the flesh are, we do well to not shame ourselves for them, for shame will never get us anywhere. They certainly don't rank up there with pride and self-righteousness, against which Jesus spends his harshest words. But as sins of the flesh, they remain a problem. The more we fixate on the material, on food and drink, and on sexual pleasure, the more our hearts will remain small, leaving less and less room for the one who can fill them with love.

THE WORLD

While "the world" can be construed as "worldly" in the sense of material and pleasurable acquisitions, the second temptation of Jesus brings a specific focus for our consideration here:

> Then the devil took him up and revealed to him all
> the kingdoms of the world in a moment of time.
> "I will give you the glory of these kingdoms and
> authority over them," the devil said, "because they
> are mine to give to anyone I please. I will give it all
> to you if you will worship me."
> LUKE 4:5-7

The issues are "glory" and "authority."

Similar to what fuels the sins of the flesh, glory and authority are divine gifts. We are to glorify and honor people worthy of glory and honor. Just rulers. Father and mother. Anyone who excels in some art or skill. And really, just about anyone—for we all retain at least some shred of the image of God and even that shred deserves to be honored.

As for authority, there is no just society without various levels of authority, from magistrates to teachers to parents.

So when we talk about the temptation of "the world," we're talking about an inordinate grasping after honor and power. This temptation is grounded in other sins, envy and jealousy (and ultimately pride), which means that no one with honor and glory should fight to retain their status, and those who lack honor and authority should not seek it. It's that simple, right?

Well, in a democracy, it isn't that simple, because to run for office is explicitly to run to gain some power and by extension some glory. It's not that simple in a capitalist economy, because to create wealth and security for one's loved ones is to seek to have power over life's contingencies. It's not that simple in the family, where the decision to have children is the decision to have authority over them. And on it goes.

So we're not talking about outward behavior when we're talking about eschewing glory and authority. We're talking about the motive in the human heart.

How do we ensure better motives? What comes first and last is confession: acknowledging that this is a temptation already lodged in our hearts and is not likely to go away anytime soon. If the first sin was an act of gluttony, it was also seeking after glory.

Glory can take many forms. It's not just about honor for

honor's sake. It can be a desire for superior and unexcelled knowledge or skill, for which one will be given honor. In the case of Eve, it was a desire for unexcelled wisdom. The serpent's temptation gets right to the heart of it: "God knows that your eyes will be opened as soon as you eat it, and you will be like God, knowing both good and evil" (Genesis 3:5). As does Eve's response: "The woman was convinced. She saw that the tree was beautiful and its fruit looked delicious, and she wanted the wisdom it would give her. So she took some of the fruit and ate it" (verse 6).

This original sin, precisely because it is the root sin, is also a perennial sin of special and subtle power. I believe it touches every one of us in one way or another. It is a rare individual who can shake the yearning for excessive honor. Even when we try to eschew it, it comes at us another way.

For example, once in a while we stumble in journalism, and one of my jobs is to apologize in writing when *Christianity Today* has published something, usually in a rush, that unnecessarily offends a group or badly misstates some facts. This happens rarely, but when it does, it's my job as editor in chief to issue an apology. Here's the thing: I receive a lot of praise for admitting that we misused our publishing platform—and so I gain some honor! I think this is silly, but I won't deny it feels good to be told by others that I'm humble. Such is the sad, sad state of the human heart.

So the place to begin shaping our motives is to recognize and acknowledge that most of the time they are mixed. I've had friends who won't take a promotion because they are unsure that they will handle their newfound authority well.

Perhaps that is a good move for some. But if we wait around for pure motives, we'll never take up any new responsibility. Rather, we might pray, "Lord, I know I'm going to like having authority and power, and I already repent of this. But help me stay in check."

And then when you are exercising authority day in and day out, and receiving honor for your good work regularly, acknowledge to yourself (and to others when appropriate) that in addition to motives of love and service, you know there is a fair amount of pride in there as well. We live by grace. And God blesses our work of mixed motives in grace. Otherwise we'd all be doomed.

The paradox is that when we admit that pride takes up inordinate space in our hearts, that's when God can find more room for himself in our hearts.

RELIGION

We should note especially the way the devil introduces two of the temptations. Before the first and third temptation, he says to Jesus, "If you are the Son of God . . ." This temptation is twofold. It's a temptation to abandon faith and a temptation to prove faith. More to the point, the first is the temptation of despair, and the second is the temptation to abandon God.

As to the first temptation, when we enter into an effort to love God wholeheartedly, a little voice in our head will start whispering, "What makes you think this is possible for a person like you? You are but a common, ordinary, run-of-the-mill human being who is weak and steadily inconsistent. And those besetting sins—do you really think you'll ever set them aside? When it comes down to it, are you really a child of God? Wouldn't it be more honest to say you are anything but?"

In short, we're talking about the little voice that wants us to deny our core identity as sons and daughters of God.

We reply boldly in the language of grace and forgiveness, "Christians aren't perfect but only forgiven!"

To which the voice replies, "Surely the so-called power of God in your life should make some difference. But there are those besetting sins, which just keep on coming, and you keep on welcoming them. Can you honestly believe in divine forgiveness when, by looking at your life, it appears you don't care one whit?"

When you begin to wholeheartedly seek God, this is what's going to happen. You are going to fail at following his will more than ever. I don't know that you will actually sin more than ever, but you will notice more than ever the ways in which you fail God. And that will make you question your sincerity. That will make you question your identity. That will tempt you with despair.

There is a prayer of dedication attributed to St. Benedict that I absolutely love precisely because it pinpoints the areas where my life needs the most attention. It's a long prayer. By the time I am done praying it, I am more keenly aware than ever of how many ways I fail God every day. But here is the line that cinches it for me. The prayer ends, "I pledge myself . . . never to despair of your mercy, O God of Mercy. Amen."

That is the line to pray when this sort of whispering begins, because we cannot will our faith in God's mercy but can only pray that he will sustain us in his mercy and then, even if we feel unworthy, live as if we are in, with, and under his mercy.

The second temptation that arises with "If you are the Son of God . . ." is the attempt to prove faith. Jesus is asked to do a miracle. We know well enough that is not in our power. But there is one thing we can do to prove our faith: we can become more religious. We can pray daily. We can worship weekly. We can memorize Scripture. We can serve at the food closet. We can witness to our friends. We can fast from time to time. We can serve on the church board. We can raise our hands in worship. We can read books about learning to love God!

Let me just say that as a Christian in the Anglican tradition, I know a lot about how ritual and tradition, ceremony, and habitual devotions can deepen love for God. I also know how they can be used to keep God at a distance. Formal prayer can be beautiful, but it can also remain merely formal, where you find yourself just muttering words you no longer think about.

And it's not a matter of working yourself up in a devotional mood when you recite written prayers, just to prove to yourself that you really mean it. I've seen some Anglicans do this sort of thing. It's no better than doing things by rote. Both can be done in a way that suggests we're trying to justify our existence, trying to prove to ourselves and maybe others that we really do believe.

Our faith is not something subject to proof, certainly not proof that would convince others, let alone ourselves. We do not have the power to convince ourselves that we have faith, that we are children of God, beloved of the Merciful One. Only God can do that. Which is why when we feel our faith is paltry at best—when that little voice plants seeds of doubt—we can pray both "Lord, let me never despair of your mercy" and "Lord, I believe; help my unbelief."

———

To reiterate (because it cannot be said too often), to embark on the journey to love God with all your heart, soul, mind, and strength is to embark on a perilous journey, strewn with potholes and dead ends, signs pointing in the wrong direction, fog and darkness, long stretches with nothing in view but a bleak landscape. Part of the reason we have forgotten God in so much of our lives is this: the world, the flesh, the devil, and religion have done a good job at erasing our memories. But ironically, the more we consciously struggle with the world, the flesh, the devil, and even religion, the more God will be a constant reality for us, if for no other reason than this: the constant prayer of our lips will be "Lord, have mercy." We are never promised that the journey with God is easy, only that, by God's grace, it is possible.

CHAPTER 14

NO OTHER GODS

ONE SIGN OF GRACE IS the law God gives as a guide to our redeemed walk with him. And the Decalogue, the Ten Commandments, is not a bad place to begin feasting on this means of grace.

One step in the long and fruitful journey to remembering God was first declared by God himself to Moses and the people of Israel: "You shall have no other gods before me" (Exodus 20:3, NRSV). This step means simply forsaking the false gods of our time and committing ourselves to the true God.

That's not easy, of course. It is complicated by the fact that it doesn't feel as if we've chosen other gods. It often seems like they have chosen us.

We are like a lone twig bobbing on the water, lazily floating down the stream—rising, falling, hopping left and right. The twig has no will but the will of the river as it meanders toward the implacable boulder that divides the current in two.

The twigs and leaves that drift to the left of the rock end up trapped in a deep pool, where the current swirls; a back current swings round again and again, creating a calm whirlpool. To the right everything borne by the water rushes on with the main current, to its final destination—a pristine lake or large reservoir or perhaps the vast and incomprehensible ocean.

From childhood, we delight in throwing twigs into a stream and watching them bob along and float away. A well-known children's film, *Paddle to the Sea*, follows a hand-carved boat as it is pulled by rivers for thousands of miles until it reaches the sea.

We're drawn to this movie as we are to watching drifting twigs, because even as children we sense that this is what life is much of the time. We are borne by a great river and bounce around as it carries us along, and we hope against hope that we'll end up someplace pristine, vast, and wonderfully mysterious.

On this journey, we approach many boulders, unsure whether we're going to be pushed to the right on to our final destination, or to the left into that back current. Many times, we sense we're stuck in the swirl, going round and round, unable to escape the futility of the eddy.

BOBBING BETWEEN TWO OPINIONS

Such was the eddy that Israel found itself in when Ahab ruled. As the chronicler of 1 Kings put it, he "did what was evil in the LORD's sight" (16:30), like the kings before him.

It started with Solomon. Though divinely warned against it, he married many wives of royal birth who worshiped other gods. Solomon had been the pillar of Jewish piety, but in deference to his wives—maybe to keep the peace, or to stop their complaining about having no decent place to make offerings to their gods, or maybe just to please them—he let himself drift with the current. He not only built altars and shrines to foreign gods, he soon found himself along with one wife or another worshiping Ashtoreth, the goddess of the Sidonians; and Chemosh, the god of Moab; and even Molech, who required the occasional child sacrifice and whom the author of 1 Kings called "the detestable god" of the Ammonites (11:7).

But it isn't as if in worshiping these other gods, he had abandoned his own. There was no thought of tearing down the magnificent Temple of the Lord he had built or forbidding the worship of Yahweh and offering sacrifices to him as well. Like a twig bobbing along left and right, he and many of his people worshiped as the current led them.

And so it went with king after king when the united kingdom was torn asunder into Judah and Israel. Jeroboam, the king of Israel, was promised the Lord's blessing if he remained faithful, but he soon found himself drifting with the current as had Solomon. In his case, it was fear that drove him.

He knew his people would regularly return to Jerusalem, the capital of Judah, to offer sacrifices to Yahweh. Perhaps they would shift their loyalty to Judah's king, Rehoboam. Jeroboam had a solution:

> So on the advice of his counselors, the king made two gold calves. He said to the people, "It is too much trouble for you to worship in Jerusalem. Look, Israel, these are the gods who brought you out of Egypt!"
>
> He placed these calf idols in Bethel and in Dan— at either end of his kingdom. But this became a great sin, for the people worshiped the idols, traveling as far north as Dan to worship the one there.
>
> I KINGS 12:28-30

On it went, back and forth, like king, like people, bobbing to the right to worship the Lord God, bobbing to the left to bow to an idol. The narrator of 1 Kings, after the reign of each king, noted the pattern by ending the narrative of each king like this: "And [so-and-so] had done what was evil in the LORD's sight (just as the family of Jeroboam had done)."

It wasn't as if Judah stayed righteous:

> For they also built for themselves pagan shrines and set up sacred pillars and Asherah poles on every high hill and under every green tree. There were even male and female shrine prostitutes throughout the

land. The people imitated the detestable practices
of the pagan nations the LORD had driven from the
land ahead of the Israelites.

1 KINGS 14:23-24

All this while the Temple in Jerusalem was bustling with
religious activity. Bobbing in the religious current, to the left
with the foreign gods, then to the right with the Lord.

Ahab drifted with the current too, only now it had become
more turbulent, like a rapid:

Ahab son of Omri did what was evil in the LORD's
sight, even more than any of the kings before him.
And as though it were not enough to follow the
sinful example of Jeroboam, he married Jezebel, the
daughter of King Ethbaal of the Sidonians, and he
began to bow down in worship of Baal. First Ahab
built a temple and an altar for Baal in Samaria.

1 KINGS 16:30-32

It was Ahab and the priests of Baal and "all the people of
Israel" whom the prophet Elijah challenged at Mt. Carmel.

Elijah's complaint was not idolatry as such. Of course
that was evil enough in the Lord's eyes. But note how Elijah
described the situation: "How much longer will you waver,
hobbling between two opinions? If the LORD is God, follow
him! But if Baal is God, then follow him!" (1 Kings 18:21).

It was the wavering, the hobbling, the bobbing left and
right—that was Elijah's complaint. The people were twigs

who had been driven by the conflicting religious currents of the day, now stuck in the swirl, going round and round, first to one god then to another, in an increasingly stagnant eddy.

Elijah's answer to this situation was to call them to a firm and resolute decision: "If the LORD is God, follow him! But if Baal is God, then follow him!"

Today we don't bow to physical idols, but when it comes to wavering, hobbling, and bobbing around—it sounds familiar. We are not complete pagans, for we worship the true God on Sunday and try to serve him as best we are able the other days of the week. But we find ourselves caught in currents that pull us along.

Perhaps the strongest current today is the so-called "information highway." But it is less like a highway that we traverse in a car whose speed and direction we control. It's more like a river that carries us along as it wills.

Many have complained rightly about the addictiveness of the Internet. But that is merely the symptom of the deeper problem: our fascination with the self. It is not an accident that the most powerful social media, Facebook and Twitter, are about curating the self we want to project for all the world to see. It is no accident that one of the first and most pervasive marketing uses of the Web was to target individuals with products and services they had already searched for. It is no accident that this medium drives people not to explore other worlds and ideas (as we thought it would) but instead leads to them withdrawing from the larger world into silos where they mostly interact with people very much like themselves and increasingly see people different from them as not merely different but immoral or evil.

This self-absorption has been criticized in many ways, depending on the critic. Allan Bloom called it *The Closing of the American Mind*; Christopher Lasch, *The Culture of Narcissism*; and others have called it the cult of self-fulfillment or rampant individualism. But these vices are actually nothing new under the sun, as a quick review of history shows. In our age, however, this constellation of self-centeredness is not considered a moral weakness, let alone a sin, but actually a virtue. In *The Ethics of Authenticity*, Charles Taylor notes,

> What we need to understand here is the moral force behind notions like self-fulfilment. Once we try to explain this simply as a kind of egoism, or a species of moral laxism, a self-indulgence with regard to a tougher, more exigent earlier age, we are already off the track. . . . It's not just that people sacrifice their love relationships, and the care of their children, to pursue their careers. Something like this has perhaps always existed. The point is that today many people feel *called* to do this, feel they ought to do this, feel their lives would be somehow wasted or unfulfilled if they didn't do it.[1]

Thus today many feel they have a moral duty to discover their "real" self—in all its gendered, racial, ethnic, political, and spiritual textures. And after discovering that self, or some part of it, they have a further duty to submit to it and to live it out.

Christians are hardly immune from all this, and like our participation in original sin, we find ourselves mimicking culture. We leave churches because "we aren't being fed." We leave spouses because "the relationship is no longer fulfilling." We stop reading the Bible because "it is boring and irrelevant to my needs." We stop praying "because I'm not getting anything out of it." We reshape moral value after moral value because we find they push against the economic, sexual, or political self we not only want to be but *feel it our duty to be*.

This is the cultural river that carries us along in our age. To be sure, we sense something deeply wrong with this way of conceiving the self and the world, and from time to time we come to our senses—yet before long we are thrown back into the middle of the rushing current.

Jesus talks about the problem in terms of God and mammon—mammon being a fill-in for any no-god. Paul talks about it as being "tossed and blown about by every wind of new teaching" (Ephesians 4:14), as does James: "Do not waver, for a person with divided loyalty is as unsettled as a wave of the sea that is blown and tossed by the wind" (1:6).

RESISTING THE CURRENT

So how do we resist the cultural current that wants to drive us in an eddy? How do we get free of the no-god of the self to worship the true God of the universe? It is a decision we each are called to make: "Repent and believe," proclaimed Jesus, "for the kingdom of heaven is at hand" (see Mark 1:15).

This decision, however, this ability to choose God comes only by a miracle of grace. For Ahab and the priests of Baal and the people of Israel, it happened like this:[2]

Elijah turned to the prophets of Baal and said, "Now bring two bulls. The prophets of Baal may choose whichever one they wish and cut it into pieces and lay it on the wood of their altar, but without setting fire to it."

Elijah, for his part, did the same. Then he said, "Then call on the name of your god, and I will call on the name of the LORD. The god who answers by setting fire to the wood is the true God!"

This was agreeable to everyone, and so the prophets of Baal began. They prepared a bull, placed it on an altar, and prayed, "O Baal, answer us!" They did this for hours on end, dancing around the altar.

By noon, Elijah could no longer contain himself and began mocking them: "You'll have to shout louder, for surely he is a god! Perhaps he is daydreaming, or is relieving himself. Or maybe he is away on a trip, or is asleep and needs to be wakened!"

At this, the prophets of Baal started shouting their prayers louder, and as this ritual required, they cut themselves until blood flowed from their veins. All to no avail, as by evening there was, as the narrator of 1 Kings put it, "no sound, no reply, no response."

Then Elijah told the people to come to his altar. It wasn't

much to look at; it was an ancient altar that had been torn down. So first he rebuilt it with twelve stones, one for each tribe of Israel. Then he dug a trench around it, enough to hold three gallons of water. Then he placed wood on the altar, cut the bull into pieces, and laid the pieces on top of the wood.

Then he said some from the crowd should fill four large jars of water and pour it over the wood and the offering.

When they had done this, he said, "Do the same thing again!"

And when they finished, he said, "Now do it a third time!" With this, the water had soaked the wood and filled the trench.

Then Elijah prayed, "O Lord, God of Abraham, Isaac, and Jacob, prove today that you are God in Israel and that I am your servant. Prove that I have done all this at your command. O Lord, answer me! Answer me so these people will know that you, O Lord, are God and that you have brought them back to yourself."

And that's when the miracle occurred: lightning struck the offering, consuming the bull, the wood, and even the stones, all of which turned to dust. Needless to say, the water in the trench had completely evaporated.

After what must have been stunned silence, the people fell to the ground and cried out, "The Lord—he is God! Yes, the Lord is God!"

So it was with Paul, who was struck down on the road to Damascus. So it was with John Wesley, whose heart was strangely warmed as he listened to a reading of Luther's preface to his commentary on Romans. So it is with many who experience a sudden and palpable miracle.

For most of us, the miracle is subtle, so quiet we may not even notice it. But the miracle is this: it suddenly becomes clear that we not only have a decision to make, but a decision whose consequences are momentous. It is a silent revelation that we are drifting and bobbing and that we can decide on which side of the boulder we will travel. This revelation is pure grace, pure gift—to experience that clarity, that moment. It is not something we can will but can only be given.

But whether the miracle is palpable or subtle, what comes with it is a decision. The time for hobbling between left and right is over. The time to choose whom we will serve is on us. That day is the day of salvation. That is the hour of decision. That is the time when our conversion begins, when we say, "The LORD—he is God! Yes, the LORD is God!"

To be clear: this is not a feeling, even a pious feeling. It is not necessarily a spiritual experience. The idea of giving ourselves to God in this way may strike us as foolish as well as frightening. It would not be surprising if everything inside us rebelled against this decision.

For C. S. Lewis, it was a reluctant confession:

You must picture me alone in that room at Magdalen, night after night, feeling, whenever my mind lifted even for a second from my work, the steady, unrelenting approach of Him whom I so earnestly desired not to meet. That which I greatly feared had at last come upon me. In the Trinity Term of 1929 I gave in, and admitted that God was God, and knelt and prayed: perhaps, that night, the most dejected and reluctant convert in all England.[3]

For the man with a demon-possessed son, it was a cry of inadequacy, "I believe; help my unbelief!" (Mark 9:24, NRSV).

For many of us, it's a desperate prayer, "Lord, have mercy!"

But in any case, it is the most mysterious moment in one's life, a personal decision of the will *and* the seemingly irresistible draw of grace.

To put it another way, for Christians, the key step on the way back to moral sanity—to remembering the Lord—is the daily, maybe even hourly, vow to stop serving other gods and to give ourselves anew to the God and Father of our Lord Jesus Christ.

This stands at the very heart of the Christian life. This is what makes the Christian life the daunting and delicious challenge it is. And it is the reason we know we can't do it alone but, as noted many times in this book, can only pray, "Lord, have mercy."

CHAPTER 15

REMEMBER
THE SABBATH

THE DECISION TO PUT AWAY idols is a daily decision—even an hourly decision: "I need thee; every hour I need thee," as the hymn puts it. And so it is not surprising that as the Lord God laid out what came to be called the Ten Commandments, one of the early commandments is about ordering our lives around him: "Remember the sabbath day, and keep it holy" (Exodus 20:8, NRSV).

In part, this means setting aside one day a week to worship and glorify God. I mentioned earlier that the principal means of grace by which God instills in us a deeper desire to love him are to be had in worship: in the corporate reading of Scripture, in listening to the preached Word, in participating in the sacraments/ordinances Jesus has instituted.

The more we give ourselves to these regular, even mundane means of grace, the greater God will fill our hearts. There is much more to be said about these means of grace, which I've addressed partly in another book.[1]

In this book, I want to look at the lesser known means of grace. And one implicit in this commandment has to do with ordering not merely one's Sabbath but one's entire week around the Lord. By implication, the Sabbath commandment is about ordering our days and even our hours. Those who have made even the weakest effort to devote themselves unwaveringly to God know that it takes more than weekly worship. Most of us have experienced the phenomenon: we enjoy glorious worship on Sunday, with firm vows to serve the Lord in humility and love the next week, only to return to church the following Sunday realizing we have hardly given God a second thought. This is not a formula for a transformed life.

In an unpublished manuscript, the great spiritual teacher Richard Foster notes,

> Now, our first task—our great task, our central task—
> is incarnating this reality of a with-God life into the
> *daily experience of our people* right where they live
> and work and cry and pray and curse the darkness.
> If we do not make substantial progress forward here,
> all our other efforts will simply dry up and blow
> away. The actual substance of our lives needs to be so
> dramatically different—transformed at the deepest,
> subterranean level, that everyone can see the difference
> and glorify God, who has caused the difference.[2]

This is not going to happen unless and until we figure out how to remember the Lord in the "daily experience" where we "live and work and cry and pray and curse the darkness."

And thus the sage advice given age after age that we begin each day with prayer and reflection on the Scriptures. This is good advice as far as it goes, but it doesn't go far enough. For the problem noted above repeats itself, but now on a daily basis. We begin the day with a focus on God and his will, and then we jump into our day—and we don't give God another thought until the next morning.

The psalmist shows us the way forward. He hints at it in Psalm 1, where the righteous person is described as one who "delight[s] in the law of the LORD, meditating on it day and night" (verse 2). But the psalmist's vision is not limited to morning and evening prayer. The passion is not merely that God would punctuate the day. The yearning goes deeper:

> Happy are those whose way is blameless,
>> who walk in the law of the LORD.
> Happy are those who keep his decrees,
>> who seek him with their whole heart.

PSALM 119:1-2, NRSV

And how does the psalmist prepare his heart to seek God in this way?

> Seven times a day I praise you
>> for your righteous ordinances.

Great peace have those who love your law;
   nothing can make them stumble.

PSALM 119:164-165, NRSV

For the psalmist, to meditate on the law of God night and day, to praise him for his law seven times a day—these are the equivalent of prayer to and meditation on God himself. For the psalmist, the law is the very revelation of God's character and love.

At this point, you might be thinking, *Seven quiet times a day? Are you kidding?*

The fact that part of us reacts this way suggests how far short our devotion to God falls, at least compared to the psalmist. It also reveals how we have already decided to order our lives (and how the culture has ordered our lives for us) because the next reaction is not atypical: *Who can find time for that?*

Yet there is a history of Christians shaping their lives in just the way the psalmist did. And in that history we see the fruits of that ordering. I'm referring, of course, to monasticism and the thousands upon thousands of men and women who trod that path, shaping their days around seven periods of prayer: matins, lauds, terce, sext, non, vespers, and compline. One of the keenest insights of the Reformation was that such a life of devotion did not merely belong to super-Christians; every believer is not only a priest but also a monk or a nun, and all of us can love and serve God in a passion as devoted as theirs without secluding ourselves from the world. We believe today in not only the priesthood of all believers but also the "monkhood" and the "nunhood" of all believers.

To put it another way: I contend that it is impossible to grow significantly in our devotion to God unless we make room in our lives to praise God and meditate on his law many times a day. Maybe not seven, but surely more than one.

I base this on two phenomena. First, that the most devout Christians throughout the ages have practiced what is called the Liturgy of the Hours. Second, my own experience, that is, my practical atheism. If I don't deliberately punctuate my day with times of prayer, God vanishes from my sight, sometimes for a whole day, sometimes for a whole week. I need to practice the Liturgy of the Hours like a recovering alcoholic needs to attend a daily AA meeting. Anyone who is desperate for something will do what it takes.

I am not holding myself up as an example. Since deciding some time ago that I ought to practice the Liturgy of the Hours, I have failed more times than I have succeeded. Do not follow my example. Here's how bad it gets many days.

Morning prayer is not much of a problem for me. But knowing how busy I get, I set my watch alarm to go off at 11:55 a.m. and 4:30 p.m. to remind myself to at least stop and say a short prayer if not read a psalm or two. I'd say that nine out of ten days, when those alarms go off, I am invariably in the middle of something. So I punch the "stop" button, mentally vowing to pray when I'm done with the task at hand—and then I completely forget to do it.

This is an amazing phenomenon to me. It signals a

number of realities: how our culture shapes our lives around so many things to do, how forgetful I am when it comes to the things of God, and ultimately how hard my heart is toward the things of God. I can't count the number of times I've felt annoyed when the alarm goes off because at that moment it feels like God is such a distraction from what I really want to do.

How different it is when we are passionately in love. I would be delighted if my beloved were to interrupt me any time of the day. I would look for excuses to spend time with her. The rest of my routine would pale in comparison to my desire to be with her.

But this is not my experience of God, and I daresay it is not the experience of most of us. In some ways, this is as it should be. I think it's fair to say that God actually wants us to forget about him for large parts of our day. I don't want my surgeon thinking about God when he's operating on my heart, or the pilot of the jet I'm sitting in closing his eyes in praise to God while landing the plane. We are called, after all, to love the neighbor, and to love means to give one's attention to the neighbor and to tasks that benefit the neighbor.

Yet it is fair to say that there is somewhere between the life of infatuation with God and the life of indifference to God. And it is fair to say that, as I argued in the earlier chapters, we Christians in America tend to fall on the indifference side more often than not. It wouldn't hurt us to build into our lives—to at least attempt to build into our lives—a routine that calls us back to our first love a few times a day.

A contemporary practice of the Liturgy of the Hours encourages prayer four times a day: morning, midday, evening, and just before bedtime. That strikes me as an achievable goal, although I must admit again that if I get in morning and bedtime prayer, that's a pretty good day.

Anglicans and Catholics have the most experience in this and offer resources that are of great help. It's good to realize that in the Catholic Liturgy of the Hours (each of which includes prayers, a reading from the Psalms, and other Scripture), morning prayer and evening prayer take about ten minutes each, midday and compline (before bedtime) take about five. Sometimes my "hour" amounts to a single prayer—the Lord's Prayer, for example, or the Jesus Prayer ("Lord Jesus Christ, Son of God, have mercy on me, a sinner"). Better than nothing, in my view.

We're not talking about a huge time commitment here. It's not the amount of time but the fact that our time is ordered around God that's the key. And yet as I've noted, our hearts are so hard that even this can challenge us.

As I conclude another chapter, especially one that has emphasized our action, it is well to note once again (because we so easily get confused) that this is not a matter of making you more religious or spiritual. If you find yourself proud of the amount of time or the number of times a day you've prayed, your heart has obviously missed the point. But as I said above about motives, we shouldn't be surprised if we start feeling proud of ourselves! And even this can lead us back to God, to confess and acknowledge afresh that it's his grace that drew us to pray in the first place.

CHAPTER 16

THE BIBLE
TELLS ME SO

A FEW CHAPTERS AGO, we looked at the temptation of Jesus as a way to consider the temptations that will plague those who seek to love God wholeheartedly. In that chapter I repeatedly encouraged prayer as a way to thwart those temptations. The careful reader will have noticed that I didn't mention the one way Jesus himself parried the devil: Scripture.

It should startle us that the Son of God, who had at his disposal unimaginable power to dispense with the devil, chose a seemingly prosaic method. Since when does quoting Scripture ever prove anything or solve any debate? Except when Jesus did it. It ended each and every temptation immediately. The devil knew he had been beaten each time, and the third time was the charm that made him coil back into his basket.

Even if we didn't have verses that exalted the authority and usefulness of Scripture—like "All Scripture is inspired by God and is useful to teach us what is true and to make us realize what is wrong in our lives. It corrects us when we are wrong and teaches us to do what is right. God uses it to prepare and equip his people to do every good work" (2 Timothy 3:16-17)—we'd still infer it from how Jesus used Scripture during his temptation.

As I noted earlier, we live in a paradoxical time. We have more and better Bible translations than ever, more attractive and helpful Bible reading methods than we can count, and yet biblical literacy continues to plummet. And as I noted earlier, I don't believe the problem is that the Bible is too hard to understand; it's that we really don't want to understand the Bible. To understand the Bible means to understand God. And this is something about which we are deeply ambivalent.

So let's admit up front that we really don't want to read the Bible and that the likely reason is that we don't want to meet God as he presents himself there. Once we acknowledge that, we can begin to make some progress in Scripture.

After the initial enthusiasm for engaging a new spiritual discipline wears off, it is good to recognize that Scripture will begin to seem irrelevant, offensive, repetitive, and altogether strange. This might be a clue that you are beginning to encounter the true God instead of the God of your imagination.

The God of our imagination is a nice God. Oh yes, he can be tough once in a while, but it's a grandpa kind of gruffness, nothing to be taken too seriously. He's also a God who makes us feel comfortable with our surroundings, who helps our material lives make sense. Mostly he's a God who inspires us with spiritual truths that help us feel loved and important and motivate us to be nice to other people.

The God of the Bible, the true God, is not nice, but he is loving. He is known to make us feel mighty uncomfortable under the gaze of his anger with sin. He is a God who can be counted on but not one whom we can take for granted—meaning he won't necessarily show up for us when and how we want him to show up. Sometimes he'll present himself in the fury of a storm, other times like the silent wasteland of the desert. Sometimes with a shout, and sometimes with a still, small voice. There is no telling how he'll show himself, but he will show himself. If we're not prepared to meet the true God, we may just miss him because we'll be looking for the wrong thing.

The main reason we need to read, study, and meditate on Scripture is not to be inspired or to have a weapon at our disposal for our fight with the enemy or so we can know how to live holy lives. The main reason is to know the true God and to wean ourselves off the God of our imaginations.

HOW TO READ THE BIBLE
FOR ALL ITS WORTH

If we're reading the Bible to get to know the true God, then it will dramatically shape how we read and study the Bible.

The long-standing evangelical tradition of reading the Bible and then "applying it to our lives" continues to have value. But something must come before this step. For if the Bible is mainly used to discover its lessons on how to live our lives, then the Bible becomes first and foremost a book about us. It is decidedly not that.

A new tradition in Bible reading, at least one taken up by evangelical scholars, is the historical-critical method. I've already mentioned this, but a few more words are in order. This method has been used in mainline circles for nearly two centuries now. It has helped us gain deeper understanding of God's ways, to be sure. One example is that we now have a deeper appreciation of Jesus' Jewishness and his historical and social milieu, as well as that of Paul. This has forced us to reconsider our understanding of the Old Testament and of the place of Jews in salvation history. That has gone a long way toward ridding the church of the anti-Semitism that has plagued it for centuries.

Yet the historical-critical method has two significant weaknesses. First, it requires us to focus on the historical, social, and literary aspects of Scripture, as it is designed to do, but at the expense of other important interpretive methods. I mentioned this earlier.

Second, the historical-critical method tends to create a caste structure in the church. The more it is used by teachers and pastors in lessons and sermons, the more the laity feels incapable of understanding Scripture on their own. The more the preacher says, "In the original languages this word actually means . . ." or "To understand this passage, we need to know the historical-political context of that era . . ." and so forth, the more the untrained layperson will stop reading

Scripture. *How can I possibly understand the Bible?* will be the thought. *I don't have the training my pastor does.*

Things can get tricky here because we do need men and women to be trained in the art of biblical study so they can bring the fruits of their scholarship to bear for the rest of the church. But the way the historical-critical method is bandied about, it leads to a feeling of inadequacy for lay readers. It ends up lowering their intellectual and spiritual self-esteem.

I know whereof I speak. I was well trained in the original languages of the Bible and the techniques of the historical-critical method at Fuller Theological Seminary. I employed my skills in my teaching and preaching when I was a pastor. And I witnessed just these two phenomena. I spent an increasing amount of time and energy thinking about the historical, literary, and social context of Scripture, and I can assure you it was a delight to do so. The Bible is a fascinating subject of study. But unfortunately it also trained me to read the Bible as if God were not present in it. And the more I employed the historical-critical method, the more insecure my parishioners felt about reading the Bible on their own.

It doesn't always work out this way—as long as we make our way back to the first purpose of Scripture: to teach us who God is and how we might love him more dearly. Medieval theologians first discerned that there are in fact four levels of Scripture reading, and their approach might help us today to better balance the ways we can read Scripture.

First, there is the literal reading: what the text says in the context of its original time and place. Even poetry, which traffics in metaphor, has a specific meaning in its original context. This is where the historical-critical method can help.

Second, there is the typological or allegorical reading. Because of some abuses in the history of exegesis, this method has been eschewed by many today. But we can't reject it, because it was used by the writers of the New Testament.

Their interpretation of Old Testament passages gives contemporary historical-critical scholars fits. Take the way the Gospel of Matthew uses such passages. When describing the holy family's escape to Egypt, we read, "That night Joseph left for Egypt with the child and Mary, his mother, and they stayed there until Herod's death. This fulfilled what the Lord had spoken through the prophet: 'I called my Son out of Egypt'" (Matthew 2:14-15). The reference is to Hosea 11:1, which is clearly about the rescue of Israel from Egypt. It does not pretend to be a prophecy about the coming of the Messiah. But Matthew sees Christ in it, and thus uses it to say that Christ's work, rescuing us from the bondage of sin, is like that of the rescue of Israel from the bondage of Egypt. The return of Christ to the land of Israel points backward to the liberation of Israel from Egyptian bondage and forward to the death of Christ on the cross.

This sort of thing happens time and again in Matthew and in the rest of the New Testament. For example, note Galatians 4:21-31, in which Paul explicitly states that the story of Hagar and Sarah and their respective sons Ishmael and Isaac is an allegory of the bondage of law and the freedom of grace in Christ.

So this is a legitimate way to read Scripture for us today as well.

Third, there is the moral reading, in which we discern the practical meaning, that is, how it applies to our lives.

Fourth, there is the anagogical or heavenly reading. *Anagog* is the Greek word meaning "to go up." This meaning points to the eventual fulfillment of all things in Christ. So, to take the example above, "I called my Son out of Egypt" can refer not merely to Jesus saving us from the bondage of sin but also the bondage of death—we will be rescued not only spiritually in this life but bodily in the life to come. These theological overtones are not mentioned by Matthew, but readers familiar with exegesis of the time would hear all these harmonies.

In our understandable passion to reject fanciful reading and to better understand the historical and literary context of the Bible, we have neglected aspects of reading that can help us know and love God more deeply. So this is not a call to reject historical-critical tools, but to keep them in their place. Only with a full reading of Scripture, one that includes the typological and anagogical reading, will we grow in our love and devotion to God.

This is but a sketch of how we might expand the way we read Scripture. This is not the place for a full and detailed picture. Retrieving the early church's method of Bible reading requires book-length treatment.[1] But this at least should give the reader a sense of how much richer Scripture can become if we read as did Christians in the early church and Middle Ages.

PRACTICAL MATTERS

It nearly goes without saying, then, that daily reading of Scripture is crucial. But I don't have to spend much time on this with evangelical readers, who continue to be committed to this, at least as an ideal. The only thing to say here is to repeat what I said above: when we slack off from daily Bible reading, let us not fool ourselves into thinking it is due to anything else but a desire to avoid the real God.

Another area that doesn't need much emphasis is the importance of reading the whole Bible. Again, evangelical readers are committed to this at least in ideal. There are many one-, two-, and three-year reading plans available. Beginners may want to skim through Leviticus and other books and passages that seem to have little edifying in them. But if you are interested in getting to know the real God in his fullness, then you have to commit to delving into even those parts of Scripture that seem arcane and puzzling.

Finally, when it comes to the Psalms, it is better to pray them than to read them as we do other portions of Scripture. Just as we have committed the Lord's Prayer to memory, we may also want to memorize some of the psalm prayers. Jesus seems to have done that. While on the cross, he quoted the psalm that begins, "My God, my God, why have you abandoned me?" (Psalm 22:1).

Praying the Psalms will present many challenges. It's all well and good to pray them when the tone and theme of the psalm match what you are currently experiencing—like reading Psalm 51 when feeling repentant or Psalm 27 when afraid or under pressure. But what happens when the psalm appointed for the day is complaining to God about his seeming lack of care when you are basking in God's loving embrace? Or when the psalmist praises God for his goodness when God seems absent? Or worse, when the psalm is calling for God to rebuke our enemies, even unto death—aren't we supposed to love our enemies? The challenges with praying the Psalms are many.

And yet there is a reason that monastic communities have committed themselves not only to praying through the Psalms regularly but even memorizing the entire Psalter. And that reason is this: praying the Psalms is not about us; it's about the church of Jesus Christ. When we pray the Psalms, we are praying *with* the church universal. Even if we are not in the same mood as the psalm, we can be sure there are many brothers and sisters that day who are. We are then praying with them and for them.

What about those troublesome passages that seek revenge on enemies? The Psalms are nothing if not honest about what is really going on in the human heart. In light of Jesus' teaching, indeed we should love our enemies. But honesty in prayer demands that we acknowledge that there is likely a part of us that wishes them ill. The psalmist won't let us off the hook with prematurely pious prayers for our enemies.

As in other parts of Scripture, there is a theological and Christ-centered way of reading the Psalms. Psalms of lament can be read as Christ's suffering, royal psalms as the coronation of Christ in the coming Kingdom, and psalms that pray for the defeat of enemies can be read as spiritual warfare with "the principalities and powers."

And then there is this: it is in the Psalms that we find some of the most exalted lines about yearning for God, panting after him like thirsty deer wanting a drink, seeking him diligently in his commandments, and so forth. Those psalms remind me what I am really about and redirect my wandering steps.

This is but a quick introduction to praying the Psalms. There is much more that might be said. Fortunately, there are many good books on helping us pray the Psalms.[2]

If you are getting the impression that remembering God and learning to love him afresh requires a lot of reading, you guessed right—the reading of Scripture first and foremost because this is a principal way we not only know about God but also come to know God himself. After all, we are called to love him not only with our heart and soul and strength but also our mind. But as we've seen, there is a way to read Scripture also with the heart.

CHAPTER 17

CONTEMPLATIVE PRAYER

Prayer is another topic, like corporate worship, that deserves a whole book in itself—or better, many books. Naturally, prayer is crucial for growing deeply in the love of God. For this book, however, a few words are in order regarding one dimension of prayer. It nearly goes without saying that prayer is not just speaking to God but listening as well—thoughtfully making ourselves silently present to the Lord.

For the doers that American Christians are, this is mighty difficult. We have things to do, plans to plan, dreams to dream, and we can't just be sitting around doing "nothing." But we cannot do something useful if we don't also develop the habit of doing nothing.

I'm forcing language here to make a point, for doing nothing in the presence of God is doing something, and something important. To do nothing in this context means not to force the moment into your preconceived idea of "meaningful prayer." It is to let whatever happens happen. You present yourself to the Lord in a quiet moment and simply say, "Here I am, Lord," and let it be.

Sometimes you will experience what seems to be the holy presence. A word or phrase may flash through your mind. You may receive a word from the Lord. Such things should never be taken at face value but tested in Scripture and with the counsel of fellow believers. And when they seem to be confirmed by such checks, we can be thankful.

But we can also be thankful when they are not confirmed or when nothing at all seems to happen. Because the point of putting ourselves before the Lord is to get used to the idea that we are not in charge of our lives. As people created in the image of God, of course we are to create and to love and to further the common and uncommon good—but only as people who are in the calm and caring hands of another. In those silent prayer times when nothing happens—well, that is when the most important thing is happening. We are learning to "be still, and know that [God is] God" (Psalm 46:10).

Such times often find my mind wandering to the worries and tasks of the day. When I cannot rid my mind and heart of such anxieties, I find it helpful to bring focus to my silence. Usually I repeat the ancient prayer "Holy God, holy and mighty, holy Immortal, have mercy on me." Sometimes that means meditating on a word or scene from Scripture. Other times, I step outside and meditate on the glories of creation.

This apparently was a habit of the psalmist:

> When I look at the night sky and see the work of
>> your fingers—
>> the moon and the stars you set in place—
> what are mere mortals that you should think
>> about them,
>> human beings that you should care for them?
> Yet you made them only a little lower than God
>> and crowned them with glory and honor.

PSALM 8:3-5

And:

> The heavens proclaim the glory of God.
>> The skies display his craftsmanship.
> Day after day they continue to speak;
>> night after night they make him known.
> They speak without a sound or word;
>> their voice is never heard.
> Yet their message has gone throughout the earth,
>> and their words to all the world.

PSALM 19:1-4

The point is to put ourselves in a place and frame of mind that will encourage wonder.[1]

The great theologian of the Middle Ages Thomas Aquinas defined wonder as "a kind of desire . . . for knowledge; a desire which comes to man when he sees an effect of which the cause either is unknown to him, or surpasses his knowledge or faculty of understanding." Wonder causes us to learn more about something that strikes us as puzzling or fascinating.

But it's different from mere curiosity, at least according to Aquinas. He says curiosity has a "tendency to wander . . . rushing after various things without rhyme or reason." It's not interested in knowing something deeply. It is in some ways the product of acedia (that is, sloth) in its lack of intellectual discipline.

Wonder, on the other hand, is very much connected to desire. It is the disciplined and steady desire to know something more fully or more deeply. And it generally concerns objects about which one can never learn enough or whose answers are not forthcoming without long effort. And even then, the object remains finally elusive.

Meditating on creation, then, is not merely a matter of knowing a tree's name and organic life cycle and structure. It is contemplating those parts of it that cannot be dissected and named, cannot be fathomed with statistics. In short, it is contemplating to the extent that one discovers new mysteries and wonders.

Wonder is both a physical sensation and a spiritual longing. And thus we see the heights of wonder expressed in poetry and philosophy and especially theology. It's that moment when we run out of words to describe what we are experiencing. When Paul is earnestly trying to describe the ways of God from the beginning to the end of history, he finally breaks down:

Oh, how great are God's riches and wisdom
and knowledge! How impossible it is for us
to understand his decisions and his ways!

For who can know the LORD's thoughts?
    Who knows enough to give him advice?
And who has given him so much
    that he needs to pay it back?

For everything comes from him and exists by his
power and is intended for his glory. All glory to
him forever! Amen.

ROMANS 11:33-36

Wonder requires a bit of discipline, however. We are not
comfortable remaining in a state of wonder precisely because
it is so unfulfilling. If our desire for better knowledge of the
object was satisfied, then we'd be done and move on. That's
how we deal with most desires. We hunger and thirst, so we
eat and drink until we are satisfied and then move on. We
long to finish a book to find out whodunit, and when we do,
we pick up another book.

The problem with living in an affluent society is not
wealth as such. It's that our wealth and leisure time allow us
to fulfill so many of our desires. We get in the habit of satisfying them and satisfying them as quickly as possible.

Thus our sexual temptations or the temptation of any
addiction, whether it be drugs, alcohol, or food. The source
of many addictions is unfulfilled desire—desire for love,

desire for peace, and so forth. And rather than learning to live with patient and godly desire for these good things, we cut off the process and indulge in one way or another to at least get a temporary fix.

The examples are legion, but the point is, as I noted earlier, we are all subject to the original sin of Eve: "She saw that the tree was beautiful and its fruit looked delicious, and she wanted the wisdom it would give her. So she took some of the fruit and ate it" (Genesis 3:6).

So when it comes to contemplation, we enjoy marveling at something that has moved from mere curiosity to wonder. But it doesn't take long for us to become restless. When it comes to meditating on some word or phrase in Scripture or some delight in the created order, we can shortcut the process as did Eve. We become impatient with unfulfilled desire—in this case, the desire to know. It feels weighty, even oppressive, because we can't get our minds around it.

And so we flee. Back to the ordinary. Back to things we can understand and control. Back to the "real" world. Except it's the real world that we've just left behind, and we've returned only to a land of shadows.

It's not easy to practice contemplation, to sit in wonder at the mystery of God and his creation. We cannot be expected to practice this with any facility and for any length of time given the world that catechizes us day and night to satisfy our desires, to do things that are useful, to be efficient and productive. It's not easy, but for those who yearn to pant after God as a thirsty deer pants after water or as a starving man after food, we have to learn to get used to living with unfulfilled desire. It's why learning the art of contemplation is such a crucial aspect of learning to love God.

Unfulfilled desire does not have to be the same as the experience of frustration. Frustration occurs when we demand that a desire be fulfilled according to our wishes and in what we consider a timely way. Godly unfulfilled desire is patient, and it actually relishes and lives in that desire, in the hope of the fulfillment of that desire at the right time.

An engaged couple experiences this kind of desire. It's in large part what fuels their relationship for the months before their wedding and honeymoon. They long to hold each other in bed, realizing physically what they feel emotionally. The unfulfilled but longed-for desire is the magic of the relationship during the long months preceding marriage.

This is the way in which we are called to live with unfulfilled desire when it comes to our yearning for God. To be sure, he is gracious, and he visits us with his beneficent presence now and again in this life. And in the life to come, that love will be known and experienced in ways we cannot imagine now. But given the reality of who God is and who we are—that is, God is infinite and we are finite—we will never be able to say we completely know the wonder who is God. He will always be a glorious mystery to us, one we long to know ever more deeply and yet one who always eludes our grasp. But this won't be a frustrating experience because we will be beyond making demands about how God ought to satisfy our desires, even our wonder, and instead, like the young man and woman in love, we'll let unfulfilled desire fuel our love and devotion to him.

CHAPTER 18

SUFFERING

IN THE LAST CHAPTER, I waxed eloquent about an unfulfilled desire that does not have to be frustrating. And as I noted, some unfulfilled desires can be deeply joyful as you look forward to the satisfaction of those desires.

But I have to be fair and say that there are parts of life with God that are frustrating precisely because of a righteous unfulfilled desire.

A wife yearns for intimacy with her husband, but he remains aloof and distant for years.

A young athlete in his prime gets hit by a car crossing a street and is paralyzed for life.

An African American man is pulled over by a police officer and intimidated and harassed when he has broken no laws.

Girls in Thailand are sold by their parents to pimps to become sexual toys for visiting businessmen.

An angry man enters a mosque with weapons and mercilessly murders fifty worshipers.

Desire for love. Desire for competence. Desire for justice. Desire for life. All sorts of desires thwarted by the mystery of evil that pervades the planet. We have every right to be frustrated and to cry out to God in anger. We believers have been doing this sort of thing for a long time:

> O LORD, why do you stand so far away?
>> Why do you hide when I am in trouble?
> The wicked arrogantly hunt down the poor.
>> Let them be caught in the evil they plan
>>> for others.
> For they brag about their evil desires;
>> they praise the greedy and curse the LORD.

PSALM 10:1-3

> O LORD, how long will you forget me? Forever?
>> How long will you look the other way?
> How long must I struggle with anguish in my soul,
>> with sorrow in my heart every day?
>> How long will my enemy have the upper hand?

PSALM 13:1-2

Perhaps the most heartfelt is the complaint of the prophet Habakkuk, who saw the coming destruction of his people at the hands of the Babylonians:

O Lord my God, my Holy One, you who are eternal—
    surely you do not plan to wipe us out?
O Lord, our Rock, you have sent these Babylonians
        to correct us,
    to punish us for our many sins.
But you are pure and cannot stand the sight of evil.
    Will you wink at their treachery?
Should you be silent while the wicked
    swallow up people more righteous than they?

Are we only fish to be caught and killed?
    Are we only sea creatures that have no leader?
Must we be strung up on their hooks
    and caught in their nets while they rejoice and
        celebrate?
Then they will worship their nets
    and burn incense in front of them.
"These nets are the gods who have made us rich!"
    they will claim.
Will you let them get away with this forever?
    Will they succeed forever in their heartless
        conquests?

HABAKKUK 1:12-17

In our day, such complaints lead many to despair, to a complete rejection of God. What's interesting about the biblical complainers is that they just hang in there. And generation after generation of the faithful have done the same. Why?

Reasons abound, but I'm particularly interested in the post-crucifixion reason. The faithful have endured suffering, sometimes patiently, sometimes impatiently, because they wanted to be like Jesus, and they wanted to know the heart of God.

The yearning to know and love God with all one's heart, soul, mind, and strength is more fraught with pain than we imagine. There is the pain of unfulfilled yearning. But there is also the pain of staring current reality in the face, seeing how short it falls from the goodness of God and his intentions for the world, and breaking down into tears.

Like Jesus did when he surveyed Jerusalem one day: "O Jerusalem, Jerusalem, the city that kills the prophets and stones God's messengers! How often I have wanted to gather your children together as a hen protects her chicks beneath her wings, but you wouldn't let me" (Luke 13:34).

And later, as he approached Jerusalem, he wept and said,

How I wish today that you of all people would understand the way to peace. But now it is too late, and peace is hidden from your eyes. Before long your enemies will build ramparts against your walls and encircle you and close in on you from every side. They will crush you into the ground, and your children with you. Your enemies will not leave a single stone in place, because you did not recognize it when God visited you.

LUKE 19:42-44

Most poignantly, note what he did when he stood before the tomb of his recently departed friend Lazarus: "Jesus wept" (John 11:35).

These are moments when it's ever more clear that Jesus is God incarnate, for he cares for his people and suffers with and for his people in the same way that God is described as suffering with and for them:

> When Israel was a child, I loved him,
>   and I called my son out of Egypt.
> But the more I called to him,
>   the farther he moved from me,
> offering sacrifices to the images of Baal
>   and burning incense to idols.
> I myself taught Israel how to walk,
>   leading him along by the hand.
> But he doesn't know or even care
>   that it was I who took care of him.
> I led Israel along
>   with my ropes of kindness and love.
> I lifted the yoke from his neck,
>   and I myself stooped to feed him.
>
> HOSEA 11:1-4

And when it comes to personal suffering, that is, suffering inflicted on him by others, this is what Jesus exclaims at one crucial point: "My God, my God, why have you abandoned me?" (Matthew 27:46).

Does this not echo God's words in Hosea? Is not God

lamenting in like fashion, "My people, my people, why have you abandoned me?"

If we say we want to know and love God, this is the God we are called to know and love—the God who knows the pain of abandonment and grieves deeply. If we are to know him and, more to the point, be like him, we have to paradoxically embrace a world and a life that abandons God and a world that often aches because it feels God has abandoned it. To yearn to know God is to be willing to embrace the sufferings of God.

I recognize I'm in dangerous territory here. I've studied the impassibility of God—that is, the idea that God in his essence cannot be surprised by anything, cannot be alarmed by anything, cannot feel distressed about anything, because he is perfect peace. I believe that if there is such a thing as the inner essence of God, it can't be any other way than like this.

Yet there is a great mystery here in that God not only chose to reveal himself as a God who cares, but he cares to the point of anger and cares to the point of grief. He is a God who took on human flesh and with it all the emotional texture of human life, again including anger at hypocrisy and grief at hardness of heart.

And then there is this—God determined to share in his Son the unfathomable pain of injustice and divine abandonment:

It was our weaknesses he carried;
    it was our sorrows that weighed him down.
And we thought his troubles were a punishment
        from God,

a punishment for his own sins!
But he was pierced for our rebellion,
    crushed for our sins.
He was beaten so we could be whole.
    He was whipped so we could be healed.

ISAIAH 53:4-5

The experience of the Son is forever embedded in the life of the Trinity so that today we pray not just to an all-knowing and all-powerful Creator of heaven and earth, existing in some distant metaphysical place far, far away, but we also pray intimately to one who knows us and our sufferings like no other:

> So then, since we have a great High Priest who has entered heaven, Jesus the Son of God, let us hold firmly to what we believe. This High Priest of ours understands our weaknesses, for he faced all of the same testings we do, yet he did not sin. So let us come boldly to the throne of our gracious God. There we will receive his mercy, and we will find grace to help us when we need it most.

HEBREWS 4:14-16

If it hasn't yet been clear that the journey toward desiring God is not cultivating spiritual high after spiritual high, this chapter will make it clear. This is not to deny the real and tangible moments of divine presence that bring indescribable joy. But to seek after God also means to trudge through the same dust that God has trudged through in Jesus. It means we'll never know and love the real God if we don't embrace the suffering and pain of the world he suffered and died for. It has been God's nature to partake in the suffering of his creation. According to Peter, we are designed to "share [God's] divine nature" (2 Peter 1:4). This means we are designed to share God's suffering.

This means we don't have quick and easy answers for those who suffer, let alone explanations for our own suffering. It also means we don't have to desert God in the midst of such suffering or that God has deserted us, for he is to be found in the middle of suffering, not just at the end of it.

And finally, it means that the goal of life is not to end suffering, ours or others'. If we can do so, all well and good. Much of loving our neighbors is doing just that. But on this side of Jesus' second coming, suffering will be with us always. And as long as suffering is with us, so is God. And that is where those who long for God will find themselves, sometimes working to relieve it, sometimes giving comfort in the midst of it, but more than anything simply enduring and contemplating the mystery of suffering as they share God's nature.

CHAPTER 19

CONFESSION

A LIFE DEVOTED TO DESIRING God with every fiber of our being will in the end be a life of glorious failure. It is a life of failure because the goal is humanly impossible. It is glorious because that is the way God designed it.

It is impossible because we are sinners. Since the Fall, our nature is corrupted. We remain incurably self-centered in every area of our lives. Even our religious motives are suspect a lot of the time. There is a part of us that yearns for God simply because knowing and loving him is its own reward. And there is a part of us that remains devoted because we believe God can make us better people, or because we fear judgment if we don't love him, or because we don't want to be punished for our sins—and a hundred other less-than-noble motives.

And then, as I mentioned earlier, there's that part of us that doesn't love God at all but can be said to actually hate him. For the unqualified power he has over us. For the demands he puts on us. For the fact that we can never escape him. The truth is, for fun-loving, easygoing Westerners, God seems pretty oppressive sometimes.

So the call to love God with all our heart, soul, mind, and strength does not entail a life of victory after victory, as if every day in every way we are getting better and better at loving God, climbing Jacob's ladder rung by rung, and drawing ever closer to the beatific mountaintop.

This is what it has felt like to me: the more I yearn to love God, the more I resent him. The more vows I make to desire him with all my being, the more I long to be free from him. And the more I find myself returning to him in contrition.

A great deal of a life with God is returning to the God we have just deserted. To put it another way, the bulk of a life with God is learning to believe—really believe—in grace.

It is learning that he is a God who is there before we sin and a God who is still there after we sin.

It is learning that there is no sin, even the besetting sins that come around as often as the sun rises, that God will not forgive.

It is learning that all the willpower we can muster is no match for the greediness of the human heart, let alone the wiles of the enemy.

It is learning to depend on God's grace from beginning to end.

We will never have a deep love for God or grow in our

devotion to him if we don't get it through our thick hearts that he is grace and love. Why would we ever want to strive, with all our being, for less than that?

The life of returning to God, and returning to him again and again, is called a life of repentance. We are apt to think that repentance is what characterizes the beginning of life with God or that it is to be reserved for special seasons like Lent. But we really know better. Jesus' first preached word is first not merely because it begins life with him but because it characterizes our entire life with him: "Repent, for the kingdom of heaven is at hand!"

Lest we think repentance a morbid practice of our Orthodox and Catholic brethren, recall that Martin Luther kicked off what was to become the Protestant Reformation by posting his Ninety-five Theses, the first of which said, "Our Lord and Master Jesus Christ . . . willed the entire life of believers to be one of repentance."

A DAILY RITUAL

I contend that if we really want to increase our heartfelt devotion to God, repentance must become a daily ritual. I don't mean a ritual self-flagellation or a wallowing in guilt and shame. We enter into confession because we know we're in the presence of a gracious God who loves to hear us confess. To be sure, we will feel remorse, but not the debilitating kind.

As one Catholic spiritual director put it, the Holy Spirit is a Spirit of peace, and he makes us feel a "tranquil sorrow" that makes us humble but also confident in God's grace.[1]

Self-condemnation, anger with ourselves, deep shame—
these are all works of the enemy. For the person in Christ,
we do not ever despair, even after committing a grave sin, for
we know what Christ has already done for us on the cross.

A ritual of repentance begins with confession. And confession begins with a deliberate accounting of one's day, usually at the end of the day. Here is a prayer from the Book
of Common Prayer (1979) that I have adapted and found
especially helpful after mentally recalling my daily failures:

> Almighty God, Father of all mercies, I confess that
> I have sinned against you in thought, word, and
> deed, by what I have done and by what I have left
> undone. I've not loved you with my whole heart.
> I have not loved my neighbor as myself. I am truly
> sorry and I humbly repent. For the sake of your Son
> Jesus Christ, have mercy on me, and forgive me, that
> I may delight in your will and walk in your ways, to
> the glory of your name. Amen.

I find that this alone opens me to know the grace of God
afresh, but if I'm still feeling weighed down, I read the first
part of Psalm 103:

> Let all that I am praise the LORD;
>   with my whole heart, I will praise his holy name.
> Let all that I am praise the LORD;
>   may I never forget the good things he does for me.
> He forgives all my sins

and heals all my diseases.
He redeems me from death
 and crowns me with love and tender mercies.
He fills my life with good things.
 My youth is renewed like the eagle's!

The Lord gives righteousness
 and justice to all who are treated unfairly.

He revealed his character to Moses
 and his deeds to the people of Israel.
The Lord is compassionate and merciful,
 slow to get angry and filled with unfailing love.
He will not constantly accuse us,
 nor remain angry forever.
He does not punish us for all our sins;
 he does not deal harshly with us, as we deserve.
For his unfailing love toward those who fear him
 is as great as the height of the heavens above
  the earth.
He has removed our sins as far from us
 as the east is from the west.

PSALM 103:1-12

The point of this ritual is twofold. First, it is designed to remind us of reality, especially the reality that we fall woefully short of loving God. Without daily confession, we start living under the illusion that we're doing pretty well after all. Keep that up, and soon we sound like the Pharisee in the parable who prays in the Temple, "I thank you, God, that I am not like other people—cheaters, sinners, adulterers" (Luke 18:11). Without regular confession, we begin to imagine that at heart we are not cheaters, sinners, and adulterers.

As Jesus said, it is better to enter into God's presence with the prayer of the publican: "O God, be merciful to me, for I am a sinner" (Luke 18:13). That's the type of prayer that God not only accepts but rejoices in. As Jesus put it, "There is joy in the presence of God's angels when even one sinner repents" (Luke 15:10).

The second reality is also one that needs to be repeatedly impressed upon us: that God joyfully welcomes our prayer of confession and gladly forgives. In short, this little ritual is designed to instill in us a rock-solid experience of grace.

And because the act of confession is framed and grounded in grace, this gives us the freedom to explore our sinfulness. The point is not to beat ourselves up but to teach ourselves— or better, to open ourselves up to the teaching of the Holy Spirit, who not only guides us into the truth about ourselves but also guides us in the process that helps us to grow up into the very stature of Christ.

A few years ago a friend told me about his battle with pornography. He found himself confessing this all too often. He began to think and pray more deeply about what was going on. It was not, he soon discovered, a simple problem of lust. He was also tempted because he was lonely, not for sex as much as for intimacy, and not just in relation to others but in relation to God. And as he continued to explore, he discovered there were also times when he indulged in pornography because he was angry—sometimes at his wife, sometimes at God. And on it went. He saw that at the root of a sexual addiction there were sins more profound than he had imagined. This helped him not only recognize even more deeply the grace and forgiveness of God (who of course knew the depth of my friend's sin all along), but also recognize how to pray more specifically for the deeper sins that were afflicting him. At the time he told me this, he didn't announce complete victory, but he said he was much more able to resist temptation than he had ever been.

Because he was confident in God's grace no matter what he found in his exploration, he felt free to explore the deeper and sometimes nastier dimensions of his soul. This has become a model for me to explore the deeper dimensions of my own habitual sins.

CONFESSION TO ANOTHER

Let me suggest that our private nightly confessions might be supplemented with weekly or monthly confession to a friend, pastor, or priest. This is not a tradition in many Protestant churches, but Lutherans and Anglicans still find room for it, even if just once a year when pastors and priests make themselves available to hear confessions. Some Christians have found a friend with whom they can do this, but it is the rare friend one can trust with this sort of thing. It's even hard to trust one's pastor—which is why some people find a pastor or priest of another church to confess to.

The scriptural warrant is unmistakably clear: "Confess

your sins to each other and pray for each other so that you may be healed" (James 5:16). This age-old truth has been rediscovered in our time by many recovery groups, the fifth step of Alcoholics Anonymous being the most notable: "Admit to God, to ourselves, and to another human being the exact nature of our wrong."

There is something powerful about taking the time to find the right words (without dissembling!) and saying those words aloud to another human being.

There is also this: because you will be seeing this person regularly, it gives a bit more motivation before the next meeting to attend to the sins just confessed! It's pretty embarrassing to have to return to your confessor with the same old sins over and over. Naturally, a good confessor will never berate you for failure but invite you to continue to draw near to the God who rejoices in those who repent.

And yet, let's face it, there will be some besetting sins that, embarrassment or not, we will be confessing time and time again. There is no getting around that. We're tempted to get our house in order before we see our confessor, but that is playing the game of pride. We want to be able to say, "I've defeated that sin" or "I'm making progress," which is all well and good, except confession is not a report card but a simple acknowledgment of where we have fallen short and how we are in need of God's mercy.

More to the point, it's where we are once again embedded in grace as we hear the gospel words coming from our confessor. We have to take Jesus literally at his word at this moment. During one resurrection appearance, John notes,

"[Jesus] said, 'Peace be with you. As the Father has sent me, so I am sending you.' Then he breathed on them and said, 'Receive the Holy Spirit. If you forgive anyone's sins, they are forgiven. If you do not forgive them, they are not forgiven'" (John 20:21-23).

In some traditions this is taken to mean that those in a priestly office are uniquely given this authority. I don't want to debate that. Church doctrine or not, there does seem to be greater existential power when a priest or pastor absolves the penitent.

That being said, all who are disciples of Jesus have the authority to proclaim forgiveness of sin to another. When we confess to another, we do so because we need to hear from another the words announcing our forgiveness. Just as there is a mysterious power in audibly speaking words of confession to instill in us an even deeper contrition, so there is a mysterious power in hearing audibly spoken words that comfort us in our forgiveness in Christ.

When it comes to any sin, especially besetting sins, C. S. Lewis has some wise advice. In this passage, he's mainly thinking of lack of chastity, but it applies to any sin we struggle with:

> We may, indeed, be sure that perfect chastity—like perfect charity—will not be attained by any merely human efforts. You must ask for God's help. Even when you have done so, it may seem to you for a long time that no help, or less help than you need, is being given. Never mind. After each failure, ask

forgiveness, pick yourself up, and try again. Very often what God first helps us towards is not the virtue itself, but just this power of always trying again. For however important chastity (or courage, or truthfulness, or any other virtue) may be, this process trains us in habits of the soul which are more important still. It cures our illusions about ourselves and teaches us to depend on God. We learn, on the one hand, that we cannot trust ourselves even in our best moments, and, on the other, that we need not despair even in our worst, for our failures are forgiven. The only fatal thing is to sit down content with anything less than perfection.[2]

I'm not keen on the desire for perfection, although it's a perfectly biblical idea (see Matthew 5:48!). Given the emphasis in this book, I'd rather say that the only fatal thing is to sit down content with anything less than a growing desire to know and love God. Sin is the great roadblock to that desire, and the life of repentance is the main way to get through it.

CHAPTER 20

LOVING THE NEIGHBOR WHILE LOVING GOD

IT WAS EARLY MORNING in a campground near La Crosse, Wisconsin, an idyllic spot that sits in the middle of the Mississippi River. Something happened that hasn't happened often enough, but I pray will happen more and more as I try to seek after God. I noticed a bird skimming along the field of grass before me. I assume he was picking off insects. Off to my left, I noticed through the morning fog channels of the vast and mysterious Mississippi. I saw my little white trailer to my right, and the metal fire ring before me, and the green Coleman chair I was sitting in.

And this is what occurred to me. The bird and the grass and the flowers in the grass, the Mississippi below and the cottony clouds above, all seemed alive with the love and presence of their Creator.

This also occurred to me: that the metal fire ring, the trailer and all its engineering, my car, the chair I sat in—all works of human creation—were made possible by the graciousness of our God, who has given us the raw materials to process and the intellectual creativity to imagine and the manufacturing skill to produce wonderful things, things that make the heart glad. They, too, seemed filled with the glory of God.

It was a moment when the world around, both divinely created and humanly created, became a sacrament of sorts, a means of grace, when I enjoyed the presence and love of God afresh. It wasn't the worship of creation, but it was a glorying in it.

This is an experience most of us have now and then. What I'm yearning for is an increasing awareness of God's presence, day in and day out. To seek after God is not to retreat from the world but to enter into the world and to perceive the world with the mind of Christ, to see God in, with, and under everything we see and everything we do.

Before concluding this book about recovering the vertical dimension of faith, I need to briefly talk about the horizontal. Part of that involves simply recognizing the omnipresence of God as I did on that splendid morning on the Mississippi. To explore that dimension would take another book. For the purposes of this book, I want to look at one dimension of daily life that is so important that Jesus mentioned it in the same breath in which he called us to give everything to God in love. This book is about that first commandment, but I would be remiss if I ended the book without mentioning the second, and specifically how we can see God and seek God while we love the neighbor.

Once again, we have to be grateful for the gift the American church brings to global Christianity—among other things is our American can-do and even must-do spirit. We are a practical group, and we think often about ethics, and we put a lot of Christian boots on the ground.

As with any strength, our can-do attitude can also become a weakness, and I've pointed out in various ways how the horizontal can eclipse the vertical. In some ways, this tension between the vertical and the horizontal will be with us always. In other ways, there is no tension whatsoever. As I said, Jesus himself hardly took a breath between announcing the two commandments. And we've all known people, even ourselves at times, in whom the two have been so organically connected that we hardly notice a difference.

Still, I think it fair to the reader to suggest what the love of God looks like in lives committed to loving the neighbor.

To begin with, it hardly looks any different.

That is, no matter how much we long for God and desire to bask in his love, we still have to get dressed, get the kids ready for school, get to the day's chores or the to-do list at the office. We still need to reach out to our next-door neighbors, do what we can for the homeless, work against abortion and racial prejudice, attend the Christian education committee meeting, support world missions, and so on and so forth. God has given us six days a week to love the neighbor— the neighbor in our homes, the neighbor next door, and the neighbor across the world. This book is not a call to retreat from that.

But if it doesn't *look* any different, then what is the point?

Well, the love of God is one of those things that may not look much different but makes all the difference in the world.

To be sure, it will change the shape of our outward lives to some degree. I've suggested the need to carve out two to four times a day when, for brief moments, we read Scripture and pray—sort of a coffee break for God. You'll notice yourself doing this, but hardly anyone else should.

You may end up adding a prayer retreat every few months or maybe once a year. You may get up half an hour earlier to make sure you start your day in prayer. But from the outside, I don't know that it's going to change your life all that much.

But as I said, it can still make all the difference.

For one thing, when the desire for God becomes what it should be—something pursued with every fiber of our being—it will keep our life's focus where it should be.

To get at that, let's clarify the nature of the second great commandment. It's about loving the neighbor, and in particular, loving the neighbor *as we love ourselves.* The meaning of that little phrase is surely deep and wide, but for our purposes here, I want to focus on one crucial aspect.

As I argued in the opening chapters, in the words of Augustine, our hearts are restless until they rest in God. That is, first and foremost, beyond anything else, we were created to love God with all our heart, soul, mind, and strength. Our final destiny and purpose, that which will allow us to be the persons God has created us to be, is to glorify God and enjoy him forever. Those who love themselves will give themselves—heart, soul, mind, and strength—to bring this to bear in their own lives, with full dependence on the grace of God.

If we love our neighbors as ourselves, then it seems fitting to wish that they will enter into this glorious dimension of life as well and that we will do everything in our power to help them along in this journey. To love our neighbors as ourselves means to pray and work that they might love God with all their heart, soul, mind, and strength, so that their hearts will find rest in God.

This doesn't mean that every one of us has the gift of evangelism or that evangelism is the only game in town. Hardly. Loving our neighbors gets down to some nitty-gritty details, from changing diapers to changing laws. But *as yourself* does mean that changing diapers and changing laws are not activities designed to steady the restless and wandering human heart. We can hardly claim we are loving our neighbors if the only thing we wish for them is to raise them out of poverty or to rescue them from injustice. Those are great acts of love, no question about it. But if we love them as we love ourselves, we will continue to hope and pray that they will embark on the journey to God—what they have been ultimately created for.

Again, this doesn't mean we give a tract to every person we serve at the homeless shelter or that we try to witness to the legislator whom we're trying to persuade to make abortion harder. It does mean that we know what the end game really is, what the ultimate purpose is for us and for the life of the world. And that when we return home at night, we will praise God for the things he enabled us to do that day, and then, with a yearning that continues to fill us, we'll pray, "Thy Kingdom come," when all will bask in the presence of God, glorying in the wonder of his love.

We're not responsible for saving the world but only for loving our neighbors, in whatever form that takes. But we are responsible for praying for the world and for hoping against hope that all will come into a vital and loving relationship with their Creator.

As noted earlier, this means learning to live with a certain amount of pain. We each know a lot of people we love but people with whom we may never get a chance to talk about these ultimate things. We've seen some loved ones move away from God. Others angrily reject him. Others still act like it makes no difference whether there is a god or not. For those on the journey of divine desire, this will hurt. It will make us sad. And that too is part of what it means to love the neighbor—to grieve at such times. And as I noted, this too is to participate in the sufferings of Christ.

There is one other difference that a life committed to seeking after God will make when it comes to loving the neighbor. It will keep the ultimate before our eyes.

Take for example the family. We appropriately celebrate the horizontal blessings of family life: the pleasure of intimacy, physical and emotional, with one's spouse; the joy of children; the heritage of grandchildren. Yet God also designed marriage to point beyond family to things greater.

As Paul put it, "As the Scriptures say, 'A man leaves his father and mother and is joined to his wife, and the two are united into one.' This is a great mystery, but it is an illustration of the way Christ and the church are one" (Ephesians 5:31-32). Familial love, then, is designed to enable us to love God as well.

Or take the pursuit of racial justice and reconciliation. We usually talk about such things in completely horizontal terms and usually judge whether we've accomplished these worthy goals by counting quotas or determining whether there is love between ethnic groups. Such efforts would step into a new dimension if Christ's work of reconciliation grounded our efforts. That would remind us that we don't have to work to be reconciled but only to work out the reconciliation Christ has already accomplished: "For Christ himself has brought peace to us. He united Jews and Gentiles into one people when, in his own body on the cross, he broke down the wall of hostility that separated us" (Ephesians 2:14). The difference in tone is that between salvation by works and working out salvation: the former is an impossible burden; the latter an exploration of grace. The former puts the focus on our failures and efforts; the latter is framed by the work of God in Christ. And as with the family, love of God and neighbor walk hand in hand.

The same applies to any cause or justice issue we pursue. Take abortion. The movement against it is normally referred to as being pro-life. And we often talk about the evil of abortion in terms of the number of human lives that have been sacrificed to this demonic practice. And we celebrate the number of babies saved. Yes, and yes again! But the ultimate point of saving lives is so that those lives can be joined with ours and that of the whole church in loving and glorifying God.

Take the environment. Yes, we are called to be stewards and caretakers of this earth. And we should celebrate whenever we rehabilitate an ecosystem or save a species from extinction or create an environment with fewer harmful chemicals in the food and in the air. But the ultimate goal of caring for creation is to note how all of creation points to the glory of the Creator. Creation care is, in the end, Creator care—an activity that can deepen our love for God.

It is not difficult to see how this same logic works when it comes to immigration reform, sex trafficking, homelessness, public health, raising a family, creating a business, studying science, or whatever. There is the penultimate goal, and then there is always the ultimate goal.

One is tempted to get practical here and note that the most active and vigorous Christians in the public square tend to put a great deal of emphasis on the life of prayer. That's because they've learned that you cannot serve God in the world if you're not in deep relationship with God in your soul. This is not news—well, except for those who, with enthusiasm for doing good in the world, forget prayer.

I don't want to deny this relationship and this reality. But I don't want to spend much time on it because, again, we risk making the horizontal the first commandment. That is, a devoted life with God becomes important not because it helps us love God but mainly because it gives us the will and energy to love the neighbor. God becomes a means to something else. Yet loving God is crucial in its own right for its own reasons—and it will inevitably lead us to love the neighbor. We do well to keep first things first, as did Jesus when he listed these two great commandments.

In the end, this is not a call to flag in doing good works, especially when they entail loving the neighbor. But let us not fall into the temptation of forgetting God, of managing our lives and ministries for long stretches as if he doesn't exist, as if it wouldn't make any difference if he did. At its worst, that is idolatry. At its best, it's a formula for discouragement and despair. We have been created for better things.

It's no surprise that my prayer for the coming decades for the American church, especially its evangelical wing, is that it will still be known as a people who love their neighbors in ways dynamic and sacrificial.

And yet, more than anything, my prayer is that they'll be known again as maybe even monomaniacs for God, who when pressed about the focus of their lives, will fall back on the words of Julian of Norwich: "I saw him and I sought him, I had him and I wanted him."[1]

ACKNOWLEDGMENTS

As NOTED IN THE INTRODUCTION, this book is the culmination of decades of participating in and observing the evangelical movement. I consider it one of the great gifts of my life to have been accorded the opportunity to see the movement from the unique perch of the Christianity Today ministry. I am thus indebted to Marshall Shelley, who took a gamble on a young minster in 1989, believing he could be turned into something resembling a journalist. Over my thirty years at the ministry, I've been given much grace and wise guidance by my immediate supervisors, not only Marshall (at *Leadership Journal*) but also Kevin Miller (at *Christian History*), David Neff (at CT), and then Harold Smith (when I became editor in chief). And then there are the many colleagues who have sharpened my thinking over the years, certainly no one more so than Ted Olsen, my good friend and severest editor!

Portions of this book first appeared in *Christianity Today* as a series of columns titled "The Elusive Presence." Except for some minor edits, they are reprinted here with permission.

I'm grateful to CT and for readers who have offered critiques that helped me sharpen my argument.

I've tried to note the influences on me throughout the book, but I surely have forgotten from whom or from what book I first grasped some of these ideas. I make no claims that anything I say in this book is original.

A model of patient indulgence in the whole process has been Jon Farrar, my editor at Tyndale. He signed me up for a book in 2011, and I started two different manuscripts since then, both of which I bailed on. I'm glad he liked the idea for this book; otherwise we'd still be at square one.

Jonathan Schindler took point on editing the manuscript and improved it in a number of ways. He saved me a fair amount of embarrassment and clarified my thinking at important points. His enthusiasm for the book was also a big encouragement to me.

At the very top of the Patient Indulgence Hall of Fame roster goes my wife, Barbara. Many of the ideas in this book were first tested out with her in conversation, often colored by my habitual self-righteous or exaggerated tone. Over the years, she has taught me to be more measured in my judgments and more understanding of others. As parts of this book demonstrate, she still has work to do.

NOTES

INTRODUCTION
1. Dave Tomlinson, *The Post-Evangelical* (Great Britain: SPCK, 2014), ix.
2. Brian D. McLaren, *A New Kind of Christianity: Ten Questions That Are Transforming the Faith* (New York: HarperOne, 2010), 6.
3. Mark Labberton, "Political Dealing: The Crisis of Evangelicalism," speech given at Wheaton College, IL, April 16, 2018, https://www.fuller.edu/posts/political-dealing-the-crisis-of-evangelicalism/.
4. Mark Labberton, ed., *Still Evangelical?: Insiders Reconsider Political, Social, and Theological Meaning* (Downers Grove, IL: InterVarsity Press, 2018).
5. Molly Worthen, *Apostles of Reason: The Crisis of Authority in American Evangelicalism* (Oxford: Oxford University Press, 2016).
6. Michael Spencer, "My Prediction: The Coming Evangelical Collapse," *Internet Monk* (blog), January 27, 2009, http://www.internetmonk.com/archive/my-prediction-the-coming-evangelical-collapse-1.

CHAPTER 1: MONOMANIACS FOR GOD
1. Christopher Hitchens, *Love, Poverty, and War: Journeys and Essays* (New York: Nation Books, 2004), 375.
2. St. Bernard of Clairvaux, *Commentary on the Song of Songs,* translated by Matthew Henry (Altenmünster, Germany; Jazzybee Verlag, 2016), 11.
3. St. Bernard of Clairvaux, *On Loving God*, trans. William Harmon van Allen (South Wales: Caldey Abbey, 1909), 27, Christian Classics Ethereal Library, https://www.ccel.org/ccel/bernard/loving_god.viii.html.
4. Oliver Joseph, ed., "Pascal's Memorial," trans. Elizabeth T. Knuth, revised August 2, 1999, http://www.users.csbsju.edu/~eknuth/pascal.html.
5. C. S. Lewis, *Surprised by Joy: The Shape of My Early Life* (San Francisco: HarperOne, 2017), 17, 19.
6. Julian of Norwich, *Revelations of Divine Love*, trans. Elizabeth Spearing (New York: Penguin Books, 1998), 55.

7. Augustine, *Confessions*, 2nd ed., trans. F. J. Sheed, ed. with notes, Michael P. Foley (Indianapolis: Hackett, 2006), 21.

8. Augustine, *Confessions*, 21.

CHAPTER 2: WE HAVE FORGOTTEN GOD

1. Jonathan Edwards, "A Narrative of Conversions," in *The Works of Jonathan Edwards*, vol. 1, (London: Westley and Davis, 1835), 348.

2. The previous three paragraphs are adapted from an article I wrote, "Revival at Cane Ridge," *Christian History*, Issue 45, 1995, https://www.christianitytoday.com/history/issues/issue-45/revival-at-cane-ridge.html.

3. Charles G. Finney, *Lectures on Revivals of Religion* (New York: Fleming H. Revell, 1868), Christian Classics Ethereal Library, https://www.ccel.org/ccel/finney/revivals.iii.i.html.

4. Timothy Keller, "Revival: Ways and Means," *Timothy Keller* (blog), January 10, 2011, http://www.timothykeller.com/blog/2011/1/10/revival-ways-and-means.

5. "Phoebe Palmer: Mother of the Holiness Movement," *Christian History* (blog), Christianity Today, accessed August 21, 2019, https://www.christianitytoday.com/history/people/moversandshakers/phoebe-palmer.html.

6. Walter Rauschenbusch, *A Theology for the Social Gospel* (New York: MacMillan, 1917), 95. An electronic version can be found at https://archive.org/stream/theologyforsoc00raus/theologyforsoc00raus_djvu.txt.

7. Ted Olsen, "American Pentecost," *Christian History* (blog), Christianity Today, accessed August 21, 2019, https://www.christianitytoday.com/history/issues/issue-58/american-pentecost.html.

8. John Dart, "Reverend Got Tongue-Lashing for Beliefs," *Los Angeles Times*, July 3, 1997, https://www.latimes.com/archives/la-xpm-1997-jul-03-me-9454-story.html.

9. As the tiny Apostolic Faith Church puts it still. This denomination was founded by the early Pentecostal leader Florence Crawford. In its formal insistence on tongues as evidence of the Holy Spirit, it is a minority view. But it is not uncommon to find many Pentecostals and charismatics, while eschewing this view, nonetheless acting as if tongues is the only sure sign of Holy Spirit baptism. See "The Baptism of the Holy Ghost (In Depth)," Apostolic Faith Church, http://apostolicfaith.org/library/doctrinal/article/the-baptism-of-the-holy-ghost-booklet.

10. Mark Galli, "Point of Crisis, Point of Grace," *SoulWork* (blog), Christianity Today, January 21, 2010, https://www.christianitytoday.com/ct/2010/januaryweb-only/13-43.0.html.

11. We both, by the way, came up with that phrase "practical atheist" after reading Anthony Bloom's *Beginning to Pray* (Mahwah, NJ: Paulist Press, 1970).

CHAPTER 3: RETHINKING THE CHURCH: THE PROBLEM WITH A MISSIONAL MIND-SET

1. Walter Rauschenbusch, *A Theology for the Social Gospel* (New York: Macmillan, 1917). An electronic version can be found at https://archive .org/stream/theologyforsoc00raus/theologyforsoc00raus_djvu.txt.
2. Rauschenbusch, *Social Gospel*, 95.
3. Rauschenbusch, *Social Gospel*, 131.
4. Rauschenbusch, *Social Gospel*, 143.
5. Rauschenbusch, *Social Gospel*, 135.
6. Rauschenbusch, *Social Gospel*, 120.
7. Rauschenbusch, *Social Gospel*, 144–145.
8. Emil Brunner, *The Word and the World* (London: SCM Press, 1931), 108.
9. Wilbert R. Shenk, "Lesslie Newbigin's Contribution to the Theology of Mission", *The Bible in TransMission*, Special Edition, 1998: 3–6.
10. Wesley L. Handy, "Missional Homeschooling," *A Mission-Driven Life* (blog), May 31, 2011, https://missionsforum.wordpress.com/2011/05 /31/missional-homeschooling/.
11. Christopher J. H. Wright, *The Mission of God: Unlocking the Bible's Grand Narrative* (Downers Grove, IL: InterVarsity Press, 2018), 29.
12. Wright, *The Mission of God*, 23.

CHAPTER 5: RETHINKING THE CHURCH: A MORE BALANCED DIET

1. Many articles have talked about this phenomenon. Among others, The World Bank, "Decline of Global Extreme Poverty Continues but Has Slowed: World Bank," news release, September 19, 2018, https://www .worldbank.org/en/news/press-release/2018/09/19/decline-of-global -extreme-poverty-continues-but-has-slowed-world-bank; and James R. Rogers, "What's Behind the Stunning Decrease in Global Poverty?" First Things, November 26, 2013, https://www.firstthings.com/web -exclusives/2013/11/whats-behind-the-stunning-decrease-in-global -poverty.
2. D. Michael Lindsay, *Faith in the Halls of Power: How Evangelicals Joined the American Elite* (New York: Oxford University Press, 2008).

CHAPTER 6: THE FOCUS OF WORSHIP

1. As quoted in Hans Boersma, *Seeing God: The Beatific Vision in Christian Tradition,* (Grand Rapids: Eerdmans, 2018), 14.

CHAPTER 7: WHAT EVER HAPPENED TO COMMUNION?

1. This and the previous quote are from Mark Galli, "Revival at Cane Ridge," *Christian History*, Issue 45, 1995, https://www.christianitytoday.com /history/issues/issue-45/revival-at-cane-ridge.html.

CHAPTER 8: BACK TO THE BIBLE

1. Christian Smith with Melinda Lunquist Denton, *Soul Searching: The Spiritual and Religious Lives of American Teenagers* (New York: Oxford University Press, 2009).
2. Hans Boersma, *Scripture as Real Presence: Sacramental Exegesis in the Early Church* (Grand Rapids, MI: Baker Academic, 2017), chap. 1, Kindle.
3. Boersma, *Scripture as Real Presence*, chap. 1.
4. Boersma, *Scripture as Real Presence*, preface.

CHAPTER 10: MAKING SMALL GROUPS BIGGER IN PURPOSE

1. James S. Bielo, *Words upon the Word: An Ethnography of Evangelical Group Bible Study* (New York: NYU Press, 2009), 6.
2. "Largest High Schools in the United States," Largest.org, June 16, 2019, https://largest.org/people/high-schools-us/.
3. "UCF Facts 2018-19," University of Central Florida, Accessed September 12, 2019, https://www.ucf.edu/about-ucf/facts/.
4. Michael Mack, "Lyman Coleman: Small Groups Are Much More Than an Assimilation Strategy," *Small Group Leadership* (blog), October 9, 2013, https://smallgroupleadership.com/2013/10/09/lyman-coleman-small -groups-are-much-more-than-an-assimilation-strategy/.

CHAPTER 11: SHAPING DESIRE

1. Jacob Weisberg, "We Are Hopelessly Hooked," *The New York Review of Books*, February 25, 2016, https://www.nybooks.com/articles/2016 /02/25/we-are-hopelessly-hooked/.
2. *Reclaiming Conversation: The Power of Talk in a Digital Age* (New York: Penquin Books, 2015). These comments are found throughout the book and in everyday conversation about social media.
3. Olga Khazan, "'Find Your Passion' Is Awful Advice," *The Atlantic*, July 12, 2018, https://www.theatlantic.com/science/archive/2018/07/find-your -passion-is-terrible-advice/564932/.
4. *Handbook of Prayers* (Studium Theologiae Foundation: Manila, 1986), location 3228.

CHAPTER 13: THE WORLD, THE FLESH, THE DEVIL, AND RELIGION

1. C. S. Lewis, *The Screwtape Letters* (originally 1942; this edition: New York: Harper Collins, 1996), ix.
2. "Prayer to St. Michael the Archangel," Eternal Word Television Network, https://www.ewtn.com/catholicism/devotions/prayer-to-st-michael-the -archangel-371.

3. "The Porn Phenomenon," Barna, February 5, 2016, https://www.barna.com /the-porn-phenomenon/.

CHAPTER 14: NO OTHER GODS
1. Charles Taylor, *The Ethics of Authenticity* (Cambridge, MA: Harvard University Press, 2018), 16–17.
2. The quotes from the story of Elijah are found in 1 Kings 18:20-39.
3. C. S. Lewis, *Surprised By Joy* (New York: HarperCollins, 1955), 279.

CHAPTER 15: REMEMBER THE SABBATH
1. Mark Galli, *Beyond Smells and Bells: The Wonder and Power of Christian Liturgy* (Brewster, MA: Paraclete, 2008).
2. Richard Foster, "Casting Vision Next Forty Years" (unpublished manuscript, June 2018), Microsoft Word file.

CHAPTER 16: THE BIBLE TELLS ME SO
1. Again, I recommend Hans Boersma's *Scripture as Real Presence: Sacramental Exegesis in the Early Church* (Grand Rapids, MI: Baker Academic, 2017). Other books that teach a deeper reading of Scripture are Peter Leithart's *Deep Exegesis: The Mystery of Reading Scripture* (Waco, TX: Baylor University Press, 2009) and Daniel Treier's *Introducing Theological Interpretation of Scripture: Recovering a Christian Practice* (Grand Rapids, MI: Baker Academic, 2008).
2. Eugene Peterson, *Praying with the Psalms: A Year of Daily Prayers and Reflections on the Words of David* (New York: HarperOne, 1993); Dietrich Bonhoeffer, *Psalms: The Prayer Book of the Bible* (Minneapolis: Fortress Press, 1974); and Ben Patterson, *Praying the Psalms: Drawing Near to the Heart of God* (Carol Stream, IL: Tyndale Momentum, 2008).

CHAPTER 17: CONTEMPLATIVE PRAYER
1. The following quotes from Thomas Aquinas come from his *Summa Theologica* as quoted in "Desire and Wonder: Essential Elements in Catechesis," Dominican Sisters of Saint Cecilia, April 11, 2016, https:// www.nashvilledominican.org/desire-wonder-essential-elements-catechesis/.

CHAPTER 19: CONFESSION
1. This is regularly attributed to the Catholic saint known as Padre Pio (1887-1968), but I've been unable to find an original reference. Regardless, the idea is a powerful one, no matter who said it first.
2. C. S. Lewis, *Mere Christianity* (New York: HarperCollins, 2001), 101–102.

CHAPTER 20: LOVING THE NEIGHBOR WHILE LOVING GOD
1. Julian of Norwich, *Revelations of Divine Love,* trans. Elizabeth Spearing (New York: Penguin Books, 1998), 55.